WRITE YOUR
COLLEGE ESSAY IN
LESS THAN A DAY

WRITE YOUR COLLEGE ESSAY IN LESS THAN A DAY

Elizabeth Wissner-Gross

BALLANTINE BOOKS TRADE PAPERBACKS
NEW YORK

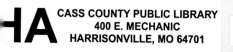

Published in the United States by Ballantine Books,
an imprint of The Random House Publishing Group,
a division of Random House, Inc., New York.

BALLANTINE and colophon are registered
trademarks of Random House, Inc.

ISBN 978-0-345-51727-2

Printed in the United States of America

www.ballantinebooks.com

4 6 8 9 7 5 3

Book design by Mary A. Wirth

To Cynthia and Robert Gross,
advocates that the fastest route is often the best route

And in memory of my father,
Irwin Wissner,
who devoted many years of his life to teaching essay-writing
to his high school English students

CONTENTS

*"How can I get through this book and finish my essay in the same day?"
you might ask. As you look through the Contents below, note that you
don't need to read every chapter of this book in order to write your main
essay. Each chapter has suggested time allotments and break allotments
too, if you're the type that enjoys racing through—but if you prefer to set
your own pace, don't feel like you have to stick with the timing indi-
cated. The second half of the book is largely devoted to how to write some
of the alternative essays and secondary essays after the main essay is
written.*

• **10-MINUTE BREAK** •

INTRODUCTION

Why You Need This Book

Overview: What You'll Find Here That You Can't Find Anywhere Else

As the creator of innovative workshops on how to write your college essay in less a day and as an author and educational strategist who has advised thousands of students seeking (and obtaining) admission into even the most competitive colleges, I am frequently asked if I know any formulas or tricks to make college application essay writing faster, better, and less painful (or even fun). The answer is, I do. Over the years, my students have produced some of the most appealing essays that have gotten them into all of the top colleges.

"What's the trick?" people ask. This book reveals my unique method—both for students able to attend my workshops, and for those who cannot. I have transformed my popular workshops for students (and teachers and counselors) into a book—this book.

My approach is based on the essays required in the Common Application, the standardized admission document that is used by almost 350 American colleges and universities. *(In fact, most of the essays written for the Common Application can be used to support an application for practically any American college that requests a personal statement or essay.)* In addition to requesting short fill-in answers, the "Common App" requires that the applicant write a "main essay" based on his or her response to one of six essay prompts:

1. Evaluate a significant experience, achievement, risk you have taken, or ethical dilemma you have faced and its impact on you.
2. Discuss some issue of personal, local, national, or international concern and its importance to you.
3. Indicate a person who has had a significant influence on you, and describe that influence.
4. Describe a character in fiction, a historical figure, or a creative work (as in art, music, science, etc.) that has had an influence on you, and explain that influence.
5. A range of academic interests, personal perspectives, and life experiences adds much to the educational mix. Given your personal background, describe an experience that illustrates what you would bring to the diversity in a college community, or an encounter that demonstrated the importance of diversity to you.
6. Topic of your choice.

Write Your College Essay in Less than a Day shows you how to respond to each of these essay prompts, to choose the subjects and wording that best represent you. Unlike other books that just show you a collection of successful essays and leave you saying to yourself, "Wow, these people have had much more exciting lives than I have had," this book helps you to see what is so intriguing and special about *your* life. And it helps you to communicate that in your essay.

I wrote this book to share my unique and easy-to-follow process that has gotten thousands of students admitted into their dream schools. Here is the gist. We are treating college essay writing like introducing you to a new sport:

1. Start with the rules: As in any sport, before you start, you'll need to know how the game is played. So before you even think about your essay topic, you'll learn some of the guidelines of application essay writing (Chapter 1). These rules are different from the regular persuasive essay-writing rules that you've likely learned in your English classes, because in addition to being convincing, these essays need to be strategic and memorable (to admissions officers). These essays need to stand out from the pack to help you reach your goal. So this book shares with you some of the lesser-known guidelines to help you write an essay that's a winner.

2. Criteria and scoring points: Once you've learned the rules, you'll want to know how to score points. In Chapter 2, you'll learn how to think like a referee—or in this case, a college admissions officer. Could you imagine playing a sport without knowing what you need to do to score points? Well, that's the approach that most students take when writing their college essays; they try to write a few things that they hope might impress the admissions officers, but they have no clear idea of what scores points. In my years of working with students, I have found that one of the most handicapping aspects of essay writing is not knowing what the college admissions officers expect of you and how you're being judged. Chapter 2 clues you in. Using an innovative and one-of-a-kind "scorecard" system that shows you what kinds of statements win points with admissions officers, you'll get to simulate the experience of *being* an admissions officer. My students have found this simulation to be both entertaining and extremely constructive. You'll read some (shortened) essays, grade them based on a unique scoring method, and choose which students get in based on the points they've earned. This will get you into the admissions-officer mind-set, so that when

you write your own essay, you'll be able to write with much more confidence, knowing how you're being perceived (and also knowing how to avoid the usual pitfalls that the vast majority of students fall into).

3. Your message: Once you are familiar with the rules, the scoring system, and the mind-set of admissions officers, you need to figure out the "message" of your application. That's the focus of Chapter 3. What is it that you're trying to tell the admissions officers? What are your "speaking points"? You need to know that before you can even pick an essay topic. This chapter helps you figure out your most appealing characteristics—the reason that colleges should want you. Just like in professional sports teams, the admissions officers only get a limited number of picks. You want to be sure that your message makes you a serious contender.

4. Your topic: Now that you know the rules, the criteria, and your message, you're ready to choose the best topic for your own essay (Chapter 4). Using the Common Application essay choices, if you select Common Application **Question 1** (recommended as the best and easiest way to produce the strongest essays in most cases), you'll learn how to find your topic in Chapter 4. If you choose instead to respond to Essay Prompt 2, the "issues" essay (geared largely for students who are community activists), you'll skip to Chapter 9. Essays 3 and 4 are the focus of Chapter 10. The good news is that you don't have to read this whole book to write your main essay, which should make it a lot easier to finish your essay within five hours.

Once you've selected your topic, you'll want to know how to structure your essay. Chapter 5 will give you the answer if you're responding to Essay Prompt 1. If you choose other essay prompts, you'll be directed later on in the book.

Throughout the book, there are loads of mini essays—good examples and clearly marked bad essays. Why include bad essays? I have found that most students learn more from mistakes—but when it comes to college application essays, it's better to learn from somebody else's mistakes than from your own. At the same time, it's also valuable to see examples of good essays. So there are plenty of those as well. Then when it's time to write your own essays, you'll know if you're on target or not.

Most applications including the Common Application require that you write a "main essay," plus a mini essay detailing one of your most important activities (Chapter 8). In addition to these Common App essays, many colleges require their own "supplemental essays" that ask you to tell the college why you want to go there (Chapter 7). Even though these essays are usually mini essays with very strict word limits, *some colleges consider these essays to be even more important than the main essays*. This book guides you through all the Common App essays, plus the supplemental Why Do You Want to Come Here? essay. (These extra essays require additional time and are not meant to be completed in the same day. But once you've completed your main essay, these shorter essays will be much, much easier and much, much faster to write.)

I wrote this book revealing my strategies because I wanted to help alleviate everyone's stress. For so many families, college application season is frenzied, and most of that tension is caused by the notion of having to summarize your entire life in 500 to 600 words. But I have found that if done correctly, the job can actually be fast and fun—as entertaining as telling one of your best friends one of your favorite stories. So my job is to share that fun with you. I aim to level the playing field for the many bright and deserving students who have limited time to devote to writing essays, who are eager to write the kind of essays that result in successful admission, and who may not have access to my essay-writing class or their own private adviser. In this book, I'm *that* adviser. I wrote this book for *you*.

NOTE TO PARENTS:

More about Why College Application Essays Are So Important

(SKIP THIS SECTION IF YOU'RE NOT A PARENT,
OR ALREADY KNOW WHY ESSAYS ARE SO IMPORTANT.)

Millions of high school seniors apply to college each year, and many buy how-to books to guide them through the application process. While grade point averages (GPA) and standardized test scores are the first factors that colleges use to determine their eligible candidate pool, these numbers still leave colleges with tens of thousands of applicants from which to choose. Add to that the fact that admissions officers at some of the most competitive colleges have advocated against relying so heavily on standardized tests to select students, claiming that the testing system is flawed. And grading systems vary so dramatically from school to school—some prestigious private schools don't even use number grades or GPAs, and increasing numbers of schools nationally don't rank their students—rendering grades difficult to interpret and an unreliable admission indicator.

So what are colleges to do? How do they ultimately choose their students?

Increasingly, students' application essays are becoming the deciding factors. In a time when fewer than one in ten applicants is getting into the most competitive colleges, the essays take on mammoth significance—effecting life-changing results—for students seeking admission into those colleges. This in turn puts tremendous pressure on each high school student applying to college—feeling the stress of having to summarize his/her life on a single page in the most meaningful, appealing, and most of all, convincing, way. Each is asked to show colleges why he/she is more deserving than tens of thousands of other applicants—and insert into these mini biographies his/her "true voice" and "personality." On top of that, most students come from homes and schools that emphasize modesty as a virtue; they're not accustomed to or comfortable with the concept of self-promotion. And few students have access to people who really know how to gain admission—or how to write the best essays—who can advise them intelligently.

Even for the most accomplished students, the application essay or personal statement can make or break the application. Entire admissions decisions are based on students' college application essays. In these competitive times when tens of thousands of wonderfully qualified students are vying for places in the most desired schools that take only 10 percent or fewer of their applicants, many of the most brilliant students get turned away from the best opportunities for lack of convincing essays. In fact, I've seen cases where much weaker students were admitted over more deserving students purely on the basis of their essays. So knowing how to communicate who you are (in addition to presenting your best grades and standardized test scores) in a one-page essay is going to give you a major advantage.

Some high schools offer in-school help: English teachers assign essay writing as part of their senior-year curriculum, and guidance counselors offer to look over these student essays. Neither necessarily is tuned in to what colleges today are looking for, but both can usually help a student to structure an essay properly. As a result, students may emerge with well-written, well-structured essays that don't get them in. Many affluent families hire private consultants to help ease the essay-writing process, and the cottage industry of college consulting has been booming in recent years. (I should note too that not all college consultants know how to craft a convincing essay—that's another reason why I wrote this book.) Yet for the vast majority of students, the job of creating an accurate but promotional autobiography is a lonely and painful task, with little helpful assistance available. As a result, the burden of having to write college application essays becomes very daunting, and in many households, a source of badgering, arguments, and hideous tension.

End the Tension Now!

Write Your College Essay in Less than a Day eliminates weeks of stress for millions of applicants and their families. Instead of leaving students to worry about the college essay alone, this book tells readers how to wrap up their essays in five hours, allowing them to get on with their lives and minimize the tension. The aim is to produce really interesting, winning, original essays—*not stock-answer or canned essays*—that are filled with personality and thoughtful insights, and that appeal to college admissions officers who read thousands of applications per year, and who find the stock essays torturous to read, and even more difficult to remember when it's time to choose students.

Won't a Five-Hour Essay Be Sloppy and Filled with Careless Errors?

Rome wasn't finished in a day—but the best college essays can be. In fact, they can be completed in a matter of hours. The most interesting application essays tend to be written in short amounts of time.

The gist of the approach is this: If the essay is torturous to write, it's generally equally torturous to read. If you want the essay to flow, then it should be told as a great storyteller would tell it, without obsessing over each word he/she speaks. Save the painstaking editing for *after* the first draft is completed. In fact, if done correctly, the toughest part of the essay process should be deciding which stories (out of an amazing array of the applicant's 16-plus years of life experience) to tell, rather than how to put together the words. Everyone has stories, and the kind of information the writer chooses to tell reveals so much about the writer. This book helps the readers find those stories that characterize themselves at their best.

Writing a 500-word essay should not be a multiday, multi-week, or multimonth process. Instead, the aim of this book is to encourage students and help them through the intimidating process in as short a time as possible—and with as much fun as possible.

In keeping with that theme, the language in the book is conversational. No big words. No overwhelming assignments. It is more of a "we're in this together" approach—coaching the reader through this tough challenge, as if his or her best friend is sitting by his/her side.

DIRECTIONS

Read This Section So You Know How to Approach This Book

Probably the most intimidating part of writing your college application essays is not knowing how you're being judged. "What is the Admissions Committee looking for anyway?" you're likely asking. This book reveals to you the kind of criteria that admissions officers use and lets you know how you're being perceived. It gives you a rubric and scorecard to score your own essays. In fact, by the end of the five hours, you too will be an expert at writing winning essays. And you will have written a most appealing essay. This book will let you know what parts of yourself to reveal, and what not to reveal, as if your best friend were right next to you guiding you all the way.

If you have to write essays and personal statements to get into college, then you might as well make it as much fun as you can. Here are some of the elements that should help make the process a little easier, more entertaining, and faster. (Note that this approach has been tried and tested and turns out really interesting and successful essays—not the "canned" essays that bore admissions officers—that have gotten students into all of the Ivies, large private universities, state universities, tech colleges, and small liberal arts colleges.)

TIMING: This book is timed. Individual chapters are timed (including the participatory activities), so you know in advance just how long it will take to get through the torture (which you may actually find to be more fun than torturous). The essay writing process should take five hours to complete (even for slow readers, and speed reading isn't necessary) including some short breaks (since the book is not written for robots). At the end of the five hours, you should have a nice solid essay that truly reflects who you are.

(Oh, and if you're one of those people who stress out over being timed, prefer to set your own pace, or don't do well under time pressure, you don't have to stick to the book's timing limits. Nobody will know or care if you go overtime.)

FUN BREAKS: Fun ten-minute breaks are built into the timing—to liven up the process, and to make essay writing a little bit more fun.

SIMULATION GAMES: Simulation games in which you therapeutically get to play the role of admissions officer—to get into the mind-set of admissions officers—are featured in Chapter 2 and again in Chapter 9. Participation is mandatory; if you don't know how admissions officers think, then you'll write the wrong essay. (So *don't* skip the role-play!)

SCORECARDS: Scorecards show you how to grade essays, so when it comes time to grade your own essay, you'll be able to estimate just how helpful it will be in increasing your odds of getting in.

BAD EXAMPLES: Readers always enjoy confidence-building bad examples of what *not* to write, and how others messed up. This book provides lots of these.

GOOD EXAMPLES: Readers also find it helpful to see some of the best examples—to get a sense of the kind of essay you want to aim for. So this book provides outstanding examples too.

INSTRUCTIONS: When reading this book, follow the order, page by page. Don't skip any chapters. Do all of the exercises. Five hours from now, you'll have a really engaging college application essay completed. And you may even surprise yourself (and your parents) about how interesting you are.

WRITE YOUR
COLLEGE ESSAY IN
LESS THAN A DAY

Start with the Guidelines
(15 Minutes)

Don't Worry about the Topic Yet—
First You Need to Know the Rules

Before you set out to write the essay, you need to know what the competitive colleges are looking for—what to write and what not to write—so you don't waste your time writing essays that will get you instantly rejected or deferred. In this chapter, you'll find most of the major rules. Read through all of them. This is really important, and it will take you only 15 minutes. After reading the rules, you'll find some sample essays—both good examples and bad. This will help you to see what colleges want and don't want. You'll notice that most of the sample essays in this book are shortened to save you time reading (your essay will be longer). You'll also notice that we keep referring to "Dreamschool College." That's the name of our pretend college in this book—the college we're all aiming for. And in case you're wondering, the mini essays used in this book are all based on composites and variations of actual student essay drafts. The following rules are listed in alphabetical order in case you want to refer to them quickly on another day.

NEGATIVE RULES

*(Or What to Avoid Writing, if You Don't Want to
Get Rejected Based on Your Essay)*

RULE 1: ADVERSITIES. Do not write about adversities that aren't adverse. If you're going to write an essay about how you have faced a risk or an adversity, make sure it's really a hardship. Not getting a brand new car for your sixteenth birthday is not an adversity. Nor is having parents who won't let you hang out with your friends on a school night, or who insist that you only attend adult-supervised parties.

RULE 2: ARTSY SUBSTITUTIONS. Do not send a poem or drawing or photo in place of an essay. If the college asks you for an essay, they want to see an essay.

RULE 3: BAD-MOUTHING. Don't write mean-spirited things about other people. Don't talk of "hating" this one or that one. Don't write in your application that you're smarter than everyone else at school, or that your principal is irresponsible, or that the guidance counselor is inexperienced, or that your whole town doesn't value education, or that your journalism teacher doesn't understand the First Amendment, or that the literary magazine adviser wouldn't know a good poem if she saw one, or that your science teacher plays favorites. High school politics should stay at high school. Don't expect sympathy from a college admissions committee.

RULE 4: BIAS. Make sure that there is no prejudice or bias in your essays. Colleges are trying hard to achieve diversity and balance among their students and faculty. Claiming or even implying subtly that you don't like this or that group is a sure way to put yourself out of the running. Don't put down others for tattoos, body piercings, sexuality, unusual hair color, race, religion, appearance, disabilities, or nation of origin. Don't refer to other people in your essays as "nerds," "geeks," "dweebs," "twits," "brainiacs," "eggheads"—even if you think you're doing so endearingly, or even if you're referring to yourself or your best friend that way. (For more about diversity and bias, see Chapter 7, The Diversity Essay.)

RULE 5: ESSAY SUBSTITUTIONS. Do not send an essay that you wrote for an English class or history class in place of the essay requested on the college application, even if you received an A on the essay, and even if your English teacher swears that it's the greatest work of literature he/she has ever seen from a high school student. Write a special essay specifically for the college application. (Exception: A very few colleges such as Union College have been known to request a graded high school paper in place of an essay.)

RULE 6: FAMILY SECRETS. Do not write about your family secrets, your friends' secrets, or even your teachers' secrets. College applications should not be treated as your big chance to tattle on the world (e.g., my teacher smokes in the faculty bathroom; my uncle thinks New Mexico is part of Mexico; my cousin deserves to go to prison; my nemesis cheated on the exam; my classmates all got drunk at the party). Tattling on the people around you makes the reader wonder how you choose your friends—and it ends up looking bad for you—even if you describe at length how you're different from your friends. This is not the place to discuss how you don't fit in with your family, or how your parents or siblings embarrass you, or how you yearn to get away from the annoying habits or rules of your household.

RULE 7: FITTING IN. Do not write an essay that presents you as "just like everyone else." Colleges are not looking to admit "everyone else." In fact, the most competitive colleges have been accepting fewer than 10 percent of applicants and rejecting "everyone else" (90 percent of applicants). Each college would prefer to find special students who specially want them for the programs and opportunities that they have to offer. In your essay, *never* refer to yourself as "a typical teenager" or even "a normal kid." If, for example, you choose to write about how you organized a car wash to raise money for hurricane victims, don't say, " . . . and we all washed cars, and we all got wet, and we all . . ." Tell the college, instead, what part *you* did that makes you stand out from the pack. Don't talk about the other kids in your "crowd" or "clique." Colleges are not necessarily impressed with kids who are confined to a crowd or clique.

RULE 8: FOOLISH RISKS. Do not write about incidents that portray you as foolhardy: taking stupid or dangerous risks that make you look accident-prone (for example, the time I got into a sky-diving accident; when I accidentally set fire to the house; wrestling with a rattlesnake; the lesson I learned from my own driving accident, etc.).

RULE 9: FRIENDS. Avoid writing about your friends and what *they* did and what *they* think. Instead, the colleges are interested in finding out more about *you* in your application. Focus solely on you. No, that won't make you sound self-centered or friendless. It will make you sound independent enough to be able to separate from your friends to attend college.

RULE 10: GIMMICKS. Do *not* send a gimmick essay (e.g., "My name is M-E-L-I-S-S-A, M is for magnificent, E is for excellent, L is for lively, I is for intelligent, S is for smart, S is for sensible, and

A is for academic." Another popular gimmick: "If I were a cookie, this would be my recipe: Lots of sugar, because I'm a very sweet person; a few nuts because I have a nutty sense of humor; a few chocolate chips made of deep chocolate, because I'm a deep thinker . . .") Gimmick essays sound flaky, clichéd, and unoriginal.

RULE 11: LOSING. Underdogs may win elections sometimes, but nobody is attracted to a total loser. Do not write an essay about losing—even if someone tells you that "losing builds character," or "it's how you lose that counts," or that it "reflects modesty," or demonstrates that you are self-effacing. Yes, everybody loses sometimes, but that doesn't mean you should devote your essay to describing your losses. You don't want the admissions officers to feel sorry for you—they never accept people out of pity. When you are competing against thousands of students who are writing about their accomplishments, the student who writes an essay that reflects self-pity probably won't be the one that admissions officers are most eager to accept. It's okay to describe tough circumstances or a rough setting, but the focus of the essay should then be how you "made good" and overcame those seemingly insurmountable challenges.

RULE 12: LUXURY VACATIONS. Do not discuss luxury resorts, cruises, sleepaway camps, or teen tours in your essays. Luxury vacations tend to be about pampering and passive activity, not character building. They're a big turnoff to admissions officers. One Ivy League admissions officer went as far as to advise students never to even mention luxury family vacations.

"Does that mean we need to hide or disguise any wealth when writing a college application?" a few wealthy students have asked. No, I tell them. You don't need to pretend not to be rich. In difficult economic times, affluent applicants may in fact seem more appealing to colleges. But writing about luxury vacations may be easily viewed as flaunting your wealth—showing off. Possible exception: If you earned your wealth on your own, independent of your parents.

RULE 13: LYING OR CHEATING. Don't copy someone else's essay—not even a sibling's, even if the sibling successfully used the essay to get into the same college you want to get into. Yes, colleges keep records; some admissions officers even remember essays. Also don't make up stories in your essays. Tell true stories about yourself. Always tell the truth; there's no need to embellish or make up anecdotes. Truthfulness is valued by colleges, as is honesty. (But don't even be tempted to write an essay about how you were honest when everyone else cheated, because that necessarily requires you to bad-mouth others, which is bad to do on your college application. See Rule 3.)

RULE 14: OLD NEWS. Do not write about an incident that happened more than four years ago, unless the incident involves you directly and has some national or international angle. For example, if you appeared on national TV to perform in a sitcom five years ago, it's okay to mention. If you made a solo violin debut at Carnegie Hall at the age of 12, it's fine to mention. If you starred in a major Hollywood movie at age 6, won a National Young Inventors Award at the age of 10, won or seriously competed in an Olympic or Junior Olympic sport, were personally invited by the president of the United States to dinner at the White House at age 8, had a nationally known choreographer review your work, or published an article in a major city newspaper at age 9—all of these are fine to mention. You get the point. No stories about learning to ride a bike, drive, ice-skate, the day the Tooth Fairy came, learning to read before kindergarten, being elected "most popular" in sixth grade, etc.

RULE 15: POLITICS. Do not discuss politics on your application. Don't try to persuade the admissions officers that you're right about politics. Don't presume that because a college has a liberal reputation or conservative reputation that the person reading your application is liberal or conservative. Admissions committees are composed of people of different ages, religions, ethnic backgrounds, physical conditions, interests, tastes, and political loyalties. An admissions officer reading your application should not be able to guess your political party affiliation by the end of the essay. And you should avoid labeling yourself as "liberal," "conservative," "right-wing," "left-wing," "libertarian," etc. A thinking person may consider him/herself conservative on one issue and liberal on another (for example, conservative about opposing underage drinking and liberal about protecting baby seals). Even if the essay prompt asks you to discuss an "issue," resist the temptation to characterize yourself with a simplistic one-word label.

RULE 16: PRANKS OR TRICKS. Do not tell stories about how you fooled, tricked, or hurt someone. Do not write essays that make you look like a bad person, even if at the end you learn your lesson and sound like a reformed person. Remember that your essay is the one opportunity you have to tell the admissions officers in your own words who you are. Don't waste that opportunity by telling them about some of the bad or worst things you've done in life. Instead, focus on the best—most compassionate, most productive, most artistic, most helpful, or most intelligent—deeds you've done and how you've already proven to be an asset to humanity.

RULE 17: RELIGION. Do not write about your religion. Do not try to proselytize or write anything that might even *sound* like you're trying to convert other people. If you even *hint* that you think your religion is better than everyone else's, you're *out*. You *may* write an essay about how you organized your youth group to feed or shelter earthquake victims. In such an essay, the bulk would focus on how you raised the money, where you collected the food, how you arranged the transportation, and how you rounded up other kids to help out. In such an essay, it's reasonable to mention the name of your church/temple/mosque/meeting house. But avoid discussing religion. In addition, you *may* write about how your church youth choir performed at the Kennedy Center in Washington or how you set up an after-school math tutoring program at your mosque or how you organized your peers from your temple to visit sick children in the hospital. In these essays, the bulk of the essay would focus on the nitty-gritty of how you led the community service—not how you helped spread your religion. There are two exceptions: 1) If you are applying to a religious college, and 2) You may also write about your interest in religion in general—*not* promoting your religion in particular—if you are applying to be a Religion major. (Example: "I have always been fascinated by the beginnings of the Church of England and its relationship to Catholicism, and am hoping to study both History and Religion in college.")

RULE 18: SEX AND DRUGS. Do not write essays about sex or drugs. Occasionally, a student will ask, "Wouldn't an essay on a taboo topic make the application memorable?" Answer: Yes, it might make the application memorable, but not in a positive way.

RULE 19: TRAVEL ESSAYS. It's okay to write about an adventure that occurred while traveling, but never list your travels in an essay. You may focus on one captivating experience that happened in a far-off place—that's fine. But never list your itinerary or the places you've visited in an essay. Although you might think it sounds very impressive to say, "In France, I went to the beaches of Normandy and visited chateaux in the Loire country, and saw Paris from the top of the Eiffel Tower, then went on to Germany to see the Rhine and to Italy to see the Coliseum," all this comes across as a laundry list, and it doesn't give the reader a sense of who you are. Anybody can copy a list of places out of a tour brochure—without really traveling at all. If you want to write about one incident while traveling, that makes a much better essay and a more engaging story (for example, hiking during an avalanche, when pirates tried to take over my cruise ship, why it took me four hours to fully absorb the Rembrandt exhibit, performing with the Metropolitan Opera Company in New York, when a bear wandered into my tent at Yellowstone, meeting my pen pal in person for the first time, lost in a foreign city, presenting my poster at the Taiwan International Science Fair, volunteering at an orphanage in India, etc.).

RULE 20: TOPIC SENTENCE. Your main application essay should *not* start with a topic sentence. Topic sentences are for English papers and history papers. The college application essay uses a completely different style. (Exceptions: The short Most Meaningful Activity essay described in Chapter 8 *may* start with a topic sentence. And the same is true for the Why Do You Want to Come Here? essay, described in Chapter 7.)

RULE 21: UNRESOLVED PROBLEMS. Americans like happy endings—even if they are sugary sweet. Never devote a college application essay to an unresolved problem. By the end of the essay, there should be a paragraph explaining the happy resolution, and possibly a moral—what you learned from the experience or how you grew. There doesn't *have* to be a moral. But there must be a happy or settled ending.

RULE 22: WHINING AND COMPLAINING. Never complain in your essay. Do not tell the college admissions officers that you're angry at your parents, you hate your siblings, and nobody understands you. Don't write about the boring environment in which you grew up—that just suggests that you're not very resourceful. (So many students write about how they are bored or unchallenged in high school—hoping to impress admissions officers that they're ready for college—but that always backfires. Bored students are, well, boring, and not likely to be actively engaged doers on campus. Colleges don't want uninspired, boring people.) Don't complain about your family's lack of wealth. Don't tell the admissions officers that you have no friends, or that you're smarter than your teachers, or that your friends have larger allowances or fancier cars. Complainers are extremely unattractive to colleges. They complain in high school, and they're likely to keep complaining in college. Colleges much prefer students who are able to appreciate the resources they are given; those are the students most likely to make the best use of the college education they are given and are likely to be engaged in activities and classes on campus.

POSITIVE RULES

Essays that are relatively fun to write—great stories that you'd enjoy sharing with a friend—are usually equally fun for admissions officers to read, as long as they don't violate any of the 22 rules listed above. Following are some additional guidelines:

RULE 1: ABBREVIATIONS. Write out all abbreviations on the first reference. Never assume that the college admissions officer is familiar with the same set of abbreviations as you are. (Instead of writing "I had summer jobs at ABP, KFC, and CPK," write "I had summer jobs at Au Bon Pain, Kentucky Fried Chicken, and California Pizza Kitchen.")

RULE 2: ACADEMIA. Try to write your essay about some episode that directly relates to your prospective college major or career ambitions. If, for example, your dream is to major in Anthropology and become an archaeologist like Indiana Jones, your essay will be much more helpful to your application if you're able to write about how you visited an archaeological site and found some interesting artifact or participated in a dig. That's much stronger than writing about how you got your driver's license or how you caught a big fish at the local pond.

RULE 3: EXPLANATIONS. If you must use complex words in your essay, explain what they mean for the benefit of the reader. If, for example, you're describing your summer's science research project on "neutrinos," explain in a few words what neutrinos are. If you want to mention some kind of machinery or software that you learned to use, don't just say, "I used an L-27." Instead, say, "I used an L-27 telescope, which is a telescope that . . ." or "I used an L-27 thermometer, which is a thermometer that . . ."

RULE 4: HUMOR. Humor can sometimes strengthen an essay— especially if the story you're telling is funny. But make sure it's funny if you're attempting to use humor. Not everyone or every situation is funny, and not everyone who isn't funny knows that he/she isn't funny. Not every sense of humor is appreciated. Sarcasm and sarcastic humor in particular generally come across very badly; they often make a student sound cranky or whiny. To learn if your humor is perceived as funny, ask a teacher who doesn't know you well to read your essay. Parents often tend to be poor judges of their own children's humor, and friends tend to be overly supportive when it comes to humor—agreeing too quickly that everything you say is funny.

RULE 5: JUDGING YOURSELF. The essays should say only good things about you. College application essays are not the places to confess your shortcomings, weaknesses, or mistakes. Yes, it's okay to say only positive things. No, that's not considered bragging. You don't have to balance the good with the bad. You should be truthful, but that doesn't mean that you have to disclose anything bad about yourself. Caution: Saying good things about yourself does not mean listing a bunch of adjectives ("I'm brilliant, creative, compassionate, and a true leader."). Instead, just tell a true story of an incident in which you were involved that demonstrates your best qualities. More on that later.

RULE 6: LEADERSHIP. The application essay is the right place to show colleges your leadership. Write about what part you led and what you did that was distinct.

RULE 7: LENGTH. The ideal length is 500 words, which fits nicely onto one page, single-spaced, but up to 600 words is usually fine too. If a word or space requirement is specified, stick to it strictly. When essays start reaching 700 and 800-plus words, they become tedious for admissions officers to read. You should be able to tell your story (or present your case) within 600 words. Realize that at some universities admissions officers read (and digest) more than 100 applications in a single day. A 1,000-word essay would slow down (and possibly annoy) the admissions officer, taking up an unnecessary amount of time, and wordy essays can be viewed as signs that the writer isn't able to write succinctly.

RULE 8: NUMBERS, QUANTIFYING, AND PROVIDING DETAILS. If you're writing about a community service you performed, a good deed that you did, or an award you won, try to quantify it (provide numbers) as best you can so the admissions officers can understand the significance of your work. Instead of saying, "I won the Beethoven Music Award," say "I won the Beethoven Music Award, which is given to the *one* top music student out of 2,000 students at Central High School by the Centerville Choral Society." Don't say, "I held a fund-raiser for New Orleans." Instead, say, "I organized a masquerade ball for Valentine's Day that raised $10,000 to help the cardiology wing of Central Hospital in New Orleans."

RULE 9: STORY. The college application essay should tell colleges who you are based mainly on one exemplary episode in your life. Choose the (high-school-age) moment that says the best things about you. (The event does not have to have occurred *in* school. An out-of-school event is just as good—or better.) Essays crammed with events tend to be the weakest (and most boring-to-read and most difficult-to-write) essays. Don't just list your credentials and achievements in a series of paragraphs. Instead, tell a true story that exemplifies you.

RULE 10: TITLE. There's no need to write a title for your application essay, although you may if you feel that a title will enhance your essay. Most students don't write titles. But if you write your essay on a separate page or attachment, make sure to label it to indicate which question you are answering.

RULE 11: VALUES. Your college application essay should echo your values, but that doesn't mean that it should be preachy. If you're writing an essay about how you collected cans of food for the hungry, you don't need to tell the admissions officer that "feeding the hungry is very important." Presumably, they know that.

RULE 12: VOCABULARY. Use your own vocabulary. Don't try to impress colleges by inserting SAT words into your essay. The simplest wording that's direct and to the point is generally the best and most interesting. Many students deliberately insert complicated words and end up using these words incorrectly. Don't go there.

RULE 13: YOUR OWN VOICE. Feel free to discuss your essay topic with others before and after writing your essay. Feel free to discuss *how* you're going to write your essay—your literary approach or style. And feel free to discuss the ideas you want to convey. But when it comes time to write the essay, *write your essay yourself*. It's fine to get editing suggestions from teachers, guidance counselors, and consultants, after the essay is written. It's fine to ask for help with spelling, grammar, style, and even ideas. But ultimately the wording should be yours. The opinions and values expressed should be yours. The experiences you describe should be yours. Together, these opinions, values, and experiences make up your "voice," and your voice is important to college admissions officers.

SO YOU'VE MASTERED THE RULES, BUT WHAT DO COLLEGES WANT?

Aside from your GPA and standardized test scores, most of what the college will know about you will come from your essays. So you have to make sure to tell them all of the things you want them to know most in the essays, regardless of the essay topics or essay questions. The gist is this: You want to tell them one of your best true-to-life stories, and you want to word it in a very direct way, as if you are telling the story to a good friend. The big difference is that somewhere in this essay (usually Paragraph 4, but we'll discuss this in Chapter 5 when we delve into the structure of the essay) you'll want to mention all of your best credentials as part of the story. College admissions officers are generally unimpressed by so-called "art essays," "personality analyses," and overly "touchy-feely essays."

THE ART ESSAY

Very, very few of the most competitive colleges want an artsy essay that fails to elaborate on who you are or why a particular college should accept you. Some students are under the misconception that an "art essay," with no particular direction, somehow sounds more intellectual and provides a better sampling of the student's artistic talents or writing abilities. This is false. Imagine that you're an admissions officer reading hundreds of essays—possibly in a single day. With each application you pick up, you ask yourself, "Now why should we accept this student? Let's see the case this student presents." If you get a rambling, descriptive, makes-no-point kind of essay, that likely won't convince you to accept the student—even if you find the description to be pleasant.

Example of a bad essay: The pure white snow blanketed the ground on the cold, crisp morning. The church steeple in the distance made the view from my window look like a New England picture postcard. The landscape was dotted with homes, and smoke daintily sprinkled out of the chimneys of some of the houses on the hills in the distance. I envisioned horse-drawn sleighs winding through the distant roads, and the absence of cars did not betray my fantasy. The trees had long since lost their leaves, so their bare branches were clearly visible, dark lines of contrast against the gleaming snow. Only the evergreens provided some colorful relief in the largely black-and-white landscape. Something rustled in the wooded area across the street. Was it a deer? No, it was two squirrels, scampering about, searching for acorns in this frosty winter wonderland. I love the peace of winter, and my idea of a great winter's day is to curl up with a book by the crackling fireplace and glance out the window occasionally to appreciate the glistening stillness of winter and the warmth inside.

"What's wrong with this essay?" you might ask. Yes, it's nicely written, but it didn't answer the essential question, "Why should we accept this student?" Yes, the setting sounds pretty and even romantic. Okay, so maybe some of it sounds clichéd and corny. But most important, it doesn't provide a single reason to accept the applicant.

Example of a better essay: As I looked outside on the cold frosty morning, I realized that my elderly neighbor was alone in her home, unable to shovel the thick snow that covered her walk. With her sidewalks icy and slippery, she was a prisoner in her own home. Struggling to break away from the novel I was reading, I showered and dressed and set out in the Arctic-like snowstorm to shovel my neighbor's walkway. I figured I could finish her driveway and my own in time to still have several hours to finish *Emma* in time for the next day's Jane Austen Book Club meeting before getting to my homework. I shoveled quickly, reminding myself of the muscles I was building and the calories I was losing by doing this deed. I hoped to complete the job and escape back to my house without my neighbor even knowing who had done this for her. But when I approached the front steps, she heard my shovel breaking the ice and came to the door. She insisted on inviting me in, and we got to talking about Jane Austen over freshly baked cookies. She showed me her vast collection of novels written by women. That's when I discovered Charlotte and Emily Brontë.

What makes the second essay much stronger than the first? The main difference is that we learn so much more about the reader, and we find some good reasons to accept her. This second essay tells us that the writer is a good person—compassionate and very thoughtful of her neighbor—willing to go out of her way to do a good deed. She shows the kind of character that we want to attract to our college. In addition, she shows us that she's intellectually interested in literature, and she's capable of enjoying an intergenerational discussion. She's not restricted to communicating with her peers; she'll interact well with her professors in college. We can envision her happily studying in a college English Department.

THE TRUE PERSONALITY ESSAY

Guidance counselors and college admissions officers advise students to make sure that their essays contain their "true personality." They say, "Make sure to let your true personality shine through." I find that most students panic when they hear that; they are at a loss as to what that means. And in response, many students get so wrapped up in trying to reveal their "true personality," that they forget to provide any interesting anecdotes or reasons that the college should accept them.

Bad example (from a complainer): My English teacher assigned us to write another "response essay" to discuss our feelings about the home and school environment in which we grew up. The truth is I hate these assignments. I'm looking forward to going to a college that will take me beyond these dumb assignments. Sure, you'll read essays by my classmates citing how inspired they are by the classes they've taken at my high school. But they won't be telling you the truth. They'll tell you that Mr. Smith's English class is the best, and then they'll hand the college essay in to Mr. Smith and get an A on it. I'm the only applicant telling you how I really feel. At our school, the classes are dull—very dull. And that's an understatement. The books they assign are boring. The homework is also incredibly boring. Each year in English, we read one Shakespeare, one Dickens, a bunch of poets, and usually another novel or two. We never get to read any suspense or action novels. I'm feeling very bored in my local surroundings. My small hometown is as dull as my English class. My parents say I've outgrown high school and this community and that I'll be much happier in college where people are much more sophisticated.

What makes this essay especially weak is that the reader gets the impression that the student is never happy. Remember: These essays are all that the admissions officers get to see of you. It's much better to write about a positive episode in your life than to use the application essay as a vehicle to complain. The same person living in a small town might choose to write the following much more positive essay:

Good example (same small town): On the way home from the school bus stop every day, I pass a drainage sewer at a curb not far from a small pond. One day, as I was walking home, I saw a large duck quacking frantically in the road right by the sewer. A bunch of ducklings clearly in her charge were on the sidewalk, safely walking in circles away from the traffic. But this big duck stayed in the street by the sewer, as if it were guarding the sewer, despite the threat of the oncoming traffic. I walked over to see if I could figure out what the problem might be. Perhaps the duck was hurt, I thought. I looked through the grating deep into the sewer and saw a tiny duckling swimming in circles in the water below. I was frightened for the wayward duckling, and could understand why the mother duck was so frantic. She had no way to rescue her baby. I realized the duck was dependent on me to swing into action. But what could I do? The duckling was at least six feet down. Fearful that the mother duck would be hit by an oncoming car, I first stopped traffic.

Then I whipped out my cell phone and called the Fire Department. Minutes later, a firefighter arrived with a long-handled net to scoop the duckling out. He thanked me for alerting him. He placed the baby duckling with its siblings safely on the sidewalk, and the mother wandered off with her crew, seemingly looking back to thank us. I live in a quiet town where people care, and it's not too much to ask a firefighter to rescue a stray duckling now and then. My dream is to become a veterinarian and possibly return to this town someday.

Notice that the second essay tells a story. The first just complains. If you had to decide which student to take, you'd likely choose the second. Does the second one reveal enough about his/her personality? Yes. Without saying, "I feel this way" or "I feel that way," the applicant makes the reader understand much more about his/her personality, character, and career plan than the first applicant.

THE TOUCHY-FEELY ESSAY

If you're going to talk disparagingly about poor conditions that you've seen or experienced, make sure to write about what you've attempted to do or what you plan to do to help fix the situation—even though you're a high school student. Do not make excuses for inaction—"being a teenager, there was nothing I could do"—that won't impress anyone. If you're old enough to apply to college, you're old enough to hold a fundraiser or make other arrangements to help find a remedy. If you don't talk of a remedy, instead of coming across as a caring, moved individual, you come across heartless, lazy, or callous.

Bad Example: On my trip to the remote village in this largely impoverished region of Africa, I was instantly greeted by the stench of inadequate sanitation. A man with no legs sat on the sidewalk leaning against a wooden shack for support, and his face looked skeletal. In fact, all of the people in this village looked skeletal, and no food was to be found anywhere. A sweet-looking child with a bloated stomach did not even bother to wave away the flies that were congregating on his face—as if he had given up on life, and the flies knew it. Apparently water was in short supply, and the residents were unable to bathe. The village had no plumbing, in any case. And I had been told that in recent years, many of the older villagers had been killed by an outbreak of disease. I never was so moved by a single day's experience. Having just enjoyed a complete buffet breakfast at the hotel, I felt a little guilty—never before had I seen such poverty. It was overwhelming and there was nothing I, as a teenager, could do about it. But it made me appreciate being an American.

Good example: On my trip to the remote African village in this largely impoverished region, I noticed that all of the people in the village looked skeletal, and no food was to be found anywhere. I leaned over and gave my apple that I had brought along in my pocket to a man with no legs who sat on the sidewalk. He accepted it reluctantly, but then he treated it as if he had been given a string of diamonds. I realized that such a token effort did not begin to meet the needs of this man or his community. So I resolved on the spot that when I would return to the United States, I would start some sort of fund-raising organization that would help feed this community. I photographed the villagers—to show people back home how severe the starvation was—and followed up the next week when I was back home. Showing the pictures I had taken to my classmates, I managed to rally together a group of 20 students to help "sponsor" this village. Just $50 per week would feed the entire village, I figured, and my next problem was to work out the logistics of how to get the food directly into the hands of the villagers.

What makes the second essay much stronger than the first is the student's action upon seeing the hungry people. The first essay describes the devastation but does not attempt to do anything about it. In contrast, the second essay reveals a student who shows genuine concern and who responds positively and energetically, setting out to attempt a true remedy. This is the type of student any college would prefer.

Now it's time to see how other application essays compare. In the next chapter, you will get to read and score twenty mini essays. By the end of the chapter, you will be an expert on which essays earn top scores—and the highest likelihood of admission.

Criteria and Scoring Points
(30 Minutes)

Your Turn to Be the Admissions Officer

DIRECTIONS: You are the Admissions Committee! To decide who gets into our college, which we are calling Dreamschool College, you'll need to read through a series of essays written by applicants. We will assume that all of these applicants have the same GPAs and standardized test scores, so they've already qualified for our applicant pool. Since our college isn't large enough for us to accept them all, their essays are going to be the deciding factors. You will find some of these essays to be very well written, and some to be poorly written. Some will demonstrate clearly that the applicant is right for Dreamschool, and some will reveal otherwise. For our Admissions Committee, your mission is to select the best applicants. Note: Dreamschool is one of the most selective colleges in America, so we will only accept 2 to 3 students out of the 20 applicants from the group (maintaining our 10 to 15 percent acceptance rate). You decide which 2 or 3 we should accept.

In order to do this, you will use the following eight criteria to score each student—to make sure you decide fairly. Expect to have a difficult time turning some applicants away. Later in this book, you will use the same criteria to score your own essays. (The criteria used are not endorsed by any one university or even based on the system used by any one university, but these criteria reflect the general values that colleges are looking for and will help you to write essays that would make you appealing—assuming you have the right grades and standardized test scores—to most universities, including the most competitive.)

1. TRACK RECORD: (20 points) Give the applicant 20 points if he/she tells you clearly what he/she is interested in and can demonstrate that he/she has started to get some experience or a track record in that field. We like candidates who *do* things and have accomplished things, and don't just talk about them. So if, for example, a student says she likes to debate and demonstrates in her application that she has already done some successful debating in high school—perhaps on the school's debate team—give her 20 points.

2. SUITABLE PROGRAM: (15 points) Give the applicant 15 points if he/she clearly states his/her interest and if our university offers a program to accommodate that interest. (For this exercise, if the student cites a specific major that he or she wants to pursue, we will assume that that our college offers that major or program.) In other words, if the student says her passion is ballet and Dreamschool offers either a dance major or a ballet company, that would provide a suitable program. If the student says he loves some activity like skydiving and we can safely presume that Dreamschool doesn't offer it, give him 0 points in this category.

3. CONTRIBUTION & DIVERSITY: (15 points) We at Dreamschool believe that a diverse campus is a much more academically stim-

ulating place. So we are looking for applicants who, in some way, enhance our college diversity or contribute some new element—academic, athletic, or artistic expertise that we don't already have. We would consider a girl who is pursuing Engineering or Physics to be contributing to diversity, for example, and the same goes for a boy pursuing Nursing or Dance.

4. FOCUS: (10 points; similar to category 2, Suitable Program) We try to attract students with a rich variety of interests, regardless of the subject of those interests, as long as the interests seem constructive, and as long as each student is able to focus on an interest or two, possibly enough to begin to develop some expertise during high school. If the applicant seems very focused, award the applicant 10 points.

5. PRESTIGE: (15 points) Are you the son/daughter of a U.S. president? Are you a famous movie star or Olympic athlete? Did you win the National Science Fair? Or have an exhibit at the National Art Museum? If you show in your essay that accepting you will bring prestige to our university, then we will award you 15 points.

6. LEGACY: (5 points) Dreamschool looks favorably on children of alums who want to attend. While those children also have to work hard to earn their own admission, we want to give them a slight boost over other candidates. If you're a legacy applicant, then we'll award you 5 points. (Legacy students earn more points on the Why Do You Want To Come Here? essay described later in this book, and have the best chances of admission by applying Early Decision to their parent's college—rather than waiting for Regular Decision, when some colleges no longer give extra points to legacy applicants.)

7. SPECIAL QUALITIES: (10 points) Dreamschool wants to make sure that all of its classes (especially less popular hard-to-fill classes) attract enough students and all of its student organizations are adequately staffed. If you offer a special quality to help fill the college's need—a harp or bassoon player for our orchestra, a female rowing champion, a student who has studied Ancient Greek in high school, etc.—we'll give you 10 extra points.

8. CHARACTER: (10 points) We want to continue to attract students of character, and assume that most of our students possess lots of character. But if you emerge from a difficult situation showing exceptional character, we'll award 10 points.

Losing Points

At Dreamschool College, like many other colleges, we like to view our applicants positively. That means we like to give students points for the good qualities that they would bring to our college instead of taking away points for qualities that a student may lack. But occasionally, we find ourselves taking away points for applications that are so poorly done or that present the candidates in such a negative light. We feel that those students are trying to tell us that they really *don't* want to get into Dreamschool. So we don't want to admit them. Following are the three criteria for subtracting points:

1. SLOPPINESS OR CARELESSNESS: (20 points) Take off 20 points if the essay is filled with spelling mistakes, typos, and grammatical errors—more than two careless mistakes—showing that the student didn't care enough about Dreamschool to look over his/her essay. Perhaps that student really prefers another college and has devoted more time to that other college's application.

2. INACCURACY: (20 points) Take off 20 points for false information or essays that contradict themselves.

3. BIAS: (20 points) Take off 20 points for anything that reveals the applicant to be offensive, prejudiced, or mean-spirited.

HANDY SCORECARD
(for main essay)

ADD points for the following:

1. Track Record	(20 points)
2. Suitable Program	(15 points)
3. Contribution & Diversity	(15 points)
4. Focus	(10 points)
5. (You Add) Prestige	(15 points)
6. Legacy	(5 points)
7. Special Qualities	(10 points)
8. Character	(10 points)

SUBTRACT points for the following:

1. Sloppiness/Carelessness	(20 points)
2. Inaccuracy	(20 points)
3. Bias	(20 points)

DIRECTIONS: Using the criteria outlined in this chapter, the rules from the previous chapter, and the scorecard provided, *you* be the Admissions Committee! You decide whom we should accept and whom we have to reject or defer.

"Why am I doing this, when I could be writing my essay?"

The idea is to learn from other people's mistakes—to know what *not* to write—and to get you into the general mind-set of admissions officers so you can better target your own essays when it's your turn to write. (You'll be able to write your essay much faster, once you know what *not* to write!)

Here is the essay question (first option on the Common Application): "*Evaluate a significant experience, achievement, risk you have taken, or ethical dilemma you have faced, and its impact on you.*" For this book, we're focusing on this essay prompt, because 1) it tends to be the most popular among students, 2) it usually turns out the best responses, and 3) it's the easiest essay to write well.

"Does this mean that if I choose a different essay prompt my odds of admission will be better, since I'd be writing on a topic that nobody else is using and that would make my application stand out?" you might ask. The answer is no. Don't choose the least-used essay prompt as a means of making your application stand out; instead choose the topic that best helps you communicate who you are. Telling about a defining experience or achievement is in most cases the best way to communicate a sense of who you are.

The following are shortened versions of how 20 applicants responded. These essays are shortened versions of actual drafts or combinations of drafts that real students have shared with me. The specific names and places have been changed to protect the students' privacy. (To help us remember each one, when it comes time for the Admissions Committee to discuss our candidate choices, we will give each candidate a one- or two-word reference name or nickname. This is not necessarily standard procedure at colleges, but this is a helpful way for our simulated committee to remember each candidate.) Under each essay is a scoring list. Grade each applicant according to the criteria on the list, to see whom you would admit if you were on our admissions committee.

You Grade the Following Applicants' Essays

1. CLOTHESHORSE: I really shouldn't be telling you this, but I don't get along with my sister. She's always borrowing my clothes and forgetting to return them, or, in the rare instance that she remembers, the clothes have stains or are helplessly wrinkled. There was the day that she got an ink stain on my prom dress. That really embarrassed me in front of all my friends—in fact, that experience was the worst day of my life, and I didn't go out for weeks after that. Getting far away from her could be very good for me for college, and Dreamschool College is very far.

		Points
1. Track Record	(out of 20 points)	_____
2. Suitable Program	(15 points)	_____
3. Contribution & Diversity	(15 points)	_____
4. Focus	(10 points)	_____
5. Prestige	(15 points)	_____
6. Legacy	(5 points)	_____
7. Special Qualities	(10 points)	_____
8. Character	(10 points)	_____
	TOTAL so far:	_____
Anything to subtract?		_____
1. Carelessness	(subtract 20 points)	_____
2. Inaccuracy	(subtract 20 points)	_____
3. Bias	(subtract 20 points)	_____
	FINAL SCORE:	_____

2. ASTRONOMER: "You should become an astronomer," John Jones, the famous Nobel Prize-winning scientist told me as we rode together on the train to Boston. (Actually, he was seated in business class, and I spotted him and asked for an autograph.) I told him about my three years of research into black holes at the Connecticut State Astronomy Laboratory and my patent for a new kind of space food, and he kindly acted impressed. Then he fielded my questions on his work on quarks and dark matter, and I was mesmerized. He suggested that I apply to Dreamschool, that Dreamschool needed more young women in Physics, and told me I had a "real future." This experience altered my entire career path.

		Points
1. Track Record	(out of 20 points)	_____
2. Suitable Program	(15 points)	_____
3. Contribution & Diversity	(15 points)	_____
4. Focus	(10 points)	_____
5. Prestige	(15 points)	_____
6. Legacy	(5 points)	_____
7. Special Qualities	(10 points)	_____
8. Character	(10 points)	_____
	TOTAL so far:	_____
Anything to subtract?		_____
1. Carelessness	(subtract 20 points)	_____
2. Inaccuracy	(subtract 20 points)	_____
3. Bias	(subtract 20 points)	_____
	FINAL SCORE:	_____

3. BASEBALL JANE: "Jane! Jane!" the fans in the bleachers screamed as I stepped onto the baseball field to pitch. I wasn't sure how the crowds would react, since I was the only girl on the boys' baseball team. I wasn't intentionally fighting for women's rights or anything. I just was looking for a challenge, and had grown up playing against the boys. The local newspapers only wanted *my* story and *my* picture when we won, though many of the boys played more impressively than I had. And despite the teasing from the boys, I had fun, and enjoyed breaking barriers.

		Points
1. Track Record	(out of 20 points)	_____
2. Suitable Program	(15 points)	_____
3. Contribution & Diversity	(15 points)	_____
4. Focus	(10 points)	_____
5. Prestige	(15 points)	_____
6. Legacy	(5 points)	_____
7. Special Qualities	(10 points)	_____
8. Character	(10 points)	_____
	TOTAL so far:	_____
Anything to subtract?		_____
1. Carelessness	(subtract 20 points)	_____
2. Inaccuracy	(subtract 20 points)	_____
3. Bias	(subtract 20 points)	_____
	FINAL SCORE:	_____

4. SURFER: As the ten-foot wave came charging at me, I remembered what my instructor had said. "Stay calm. Wait until the wave is near you. Then quickly position yourself to go with it." I followed that advice and remain alive to tell the tale. What possessed me to put myself in the ocean off the coast of Hawaii on a family vacation when I didn't know how to surf was the desire to immerse myself in adventure. (I am fascinated by physical limits and want to study physical therapy in college.) We were assured that the training was excellent, and that I'd never be in any real danger if I followed directions. Knowing that I take direction well, my parents signed me up, and there I was, ready for the ride of my life.

		Points
1. Track Record	(out of 20 points)	_____
2. Suitable Program	(15 points)	_____
3. Contribution & Diversity	(15 points)	_____
4. Focus	(10 points)	_____
5. Prestige	(15 points)	_____
6. Legacy	(5 points)	_____
7. Special Qualities	(10 points)	_____
8. Character	(10 points)	_____
	TOTAL so far:	_____
Anything to subtract?		_____
1. Carelessness	(subtract 20 points)	_____
2. Inaccuracy	(subtract 20 points)	_____
3. Bias	(subtract 20 points)	_____
	FINAL SCORE:	_____

5. INDIAN ITINERARY: The day I entered the essay contest open only to Native American high school students that featured a trip around the world as first prize, I decided I wanted to see everything. So I planned my trip. First I would visit Tibet, which is filled with interesting culture and exotic beauty. Then, I would snorkel in Australia. Next, I would visit Paris to see the Eiffel Tower. Then I would go to Rome and London, where I wanted to visit Buckingham Palace. If I had time, I would also see a fjord in Norway, before returning home.

		Points
1. Track Record	(out of 20 points)	_____
2. Suitable Program	(15 points)	_____
3. Contribution & Diversity	(15 points)	_____
4. Focus	(10 points)	_____
5. Prestige	(15 points)	_____
6. Legacy	(5 points)	_____
7. Special Qualities	(10 points)	_____
8. Character	(10 points)	_____
	TOTAL so far:	_____
Anything to subtract?		_____
1. Carelessness	(subtract 20 points)	_____
2. Inaccuracy	(subtract 20 points)	_____
3. Bias	(subtract 20 points)	_____
	FINAL SCORE:	_____

6. MESSY ARTIST: My room is a mess, but I'm a firm believer in messy rooms making creative minds—and my mind is very creative. On my desk, I have the awards I've won from the Idaho State Art Competition—the most meaningful experience of my life. I've tacked some certificates on my walls as well. And, like a typical college student, I tend to throw my clothes on the floor. "Who's going to pick up for you in college?" my mother asks, and I laugh.

		Points
1. Track Record	(out of 20 points)	_____
2. Suitable Program	(15 points)	_____
3. Contribution & Diversity	(15 points)	_____
4. Focus	(10 points)	_____
5. Prestige	(15 points)	_____
6. Legacy	(5 points)	_____
7. Special Qualities	(10 points)	_____
8. Character	(10 points)	_____
	TOTAL so far:	_____
Anything to subtract?		_____
1. Carelessness	(subtract 20 points)	_____
2. Inaccuracy	(subtract 20 points)	_____
3. Bias	(subtract 20 points)	_____
	FINAL SCORE:	_____

7. GROUNDSKEEPER: Last summer, I took a volunteer job as a groundkeeper at a resort for blind people. I vollunteered because my parents felt this would be a growth experience for me, and I wanted to peform a good deed. After a day on the job, I realised how tedous the work was. Groundkeepers were recquired to work in the tick-filled woods, and I wasn't able to use any of the resort's facilites, which had been promised to me. I fantacized about quitting, but realized how dependant the resort was on student volunteers. So, despite the total boredom, I staid the entire summer, an act that, I believe, showed character.

		Points
1. Track Record	(out of 20 points)	_____
2. Suitable Program	(15 points)	_____
3. Contribution & Diversity	(15 points)	_____
4. Focus	(10 points)	_____
5. Prestige	(15 points)	_____
6. Legacy	(5 points)	_____
7. Special Qualities	(10 points)	_____
8. Character	(10 points)	_____
	TOTAL so far:	_____
Anything to subtract?		_____
1. Carelessness	(subtract 20 points)	_____
2. Inaccuracy	(subtract 20 points)	_____
3. Bias	(subtract 20 points)	_____
	FINAL SCORE:	_____

8. FRENCH ENTHUSIAST: My family went on a vacation to Paris, which turned out to be a life-altering experience. I had never lived in such luxury before, and everyone spoke French. The food was French, as was the service. They served exotic wine with every meal. I was so impressed with French living that I decided to switch from Spanish to French when I got back to high school in the fall. Someday, I would like to return to France to visit the Riviera, but in the meantime I took the French SAT II and managed to score a 500!

		Points
1. Track Record	(out of 20 points)	_____
2. Suitable Program	(15 points)	_____
3. Contribution & Diversity	(15 points)	_____
4. Focus	(10 points)	_____
5. Prestige	(15 points)	_____
6. Legacy	(5 points)	_____
7. Special Qualities	(10 points)	_____
8. Character	(10 points)	_____
	TOTAL so far:	_____
Anything to subtract?		_____
1. Carelessness	(subtract 20 points)	_____
2. Inaccuracy	(subtract 20 points)	_____
3. Bias	(subtract 20 points)	_____
	FINAL SCORE:	_____

9. THUNDERSTORM: Ever wonder what to do if you're the tallest object at a high altitude in a thunderstorm? That's what I learned on a mountaintop one night as a summer astronomy intern. A storm moved in unexpectedly at 2 a.m.; and the thunder startled us in our tents. We had made camp in a large open field on what seemed like a cloudless, starry night. A forest ranger, who had accompanied our group, showed us how to exit the field safely on all fours. We survived, grateful to resume our sky observations the next night. And after that experience I knew I wanted to major in meteorology, which I like even more than astronomy. Next week I start my internship at the Weather Channel.

		Points
1. Track Record	(out of 20 points)	_____
2. Suitable Program	(15 points)	_____
3. Contribution & Diversity	(15 points)	_____
4. Focus	(10 points)	_____
5. Prestige	(15 points)	_____
6. Legacy	(5 points)	_____
7. Special Qualities	(10 points)	_____
8. Character	(10 points)	_____
	TOTAL so far:	_____
Anything to subtract?		_____
1. Carelessness	(subtract 20 points)	_____
2. Inaccuracy	(subtract 20 points)	_____
3. Bias	(subtract 20 points)	_____
	FINAL SCORE:	_____

10. HOMESICK: The first time I went away from home was when I was ten years old. I went to a church retreat with my Scout group. I was very homesick, and I remember crying almost the entire weekend. Nobody seemed to understand how much I missed my parents. After a while, we had a scavenger hunt. I'm not sure if the counselors let me win, but somehow, I emerged the winner. Since that experience, I haven't been afraid to go away from home and look forward to college.

		Points
1. Track Record	(out of 20 points)	_____
2. Suitable Program	(15 points)	_____
3. Contribution & Diversity	(15 points)	_____
4. Focus	(10 points)	_____
5. Prestige	(15 points)	_____
6. Legacy	(5 points)	_____
7. Special Qualities	(10 points)	_____
8. Character	(10 points)	_____
	TOTAL so far:	_____
Anything to subtract?		_____
1. Carelessness	(subtract 20 points)	_____
2. Inaccuracy	(subtract 20 points)	_____
3. Bias	(subtract 20 points)	_____
	FINAL SCORE:	_____

11. ISRAEL ITINERARY: My trip to Israel was a most enlightening and meaningful experience. My teen tour visited Masada, where ancient Jews committed suicide. Then we visited the ancient city of Jerusalem and the Wailing Wall. Then we visited Tel Aviv, which turned out to be a bustling city with an attractive boardwalk and lots of clubs. Then we visited a sample kibbutz. Then we visited an artist colony. Then we visited the caves, and they took us to Bethlehem, where Jesus was born. In addition, we went to an olive wood factory and saw Akko Prison where the old movie *Exodus* was filmed. What could be more meaningful than that?

		Points
1. Track Record	(out of 20 points)	_____
2. Suitable Program	(15 points)	_____
3. Contribution & Diversity	(15 points)	_____
4. Focus	(10 points)	_____
5. Prestige	(15 points)	_____
6. Legacy	(5 points)	_____
7. Special Qualities	(10 points)	_____
8. Character	(10 points)	_____
	TOTAL so far:	_____
Anything to subtract?		_____
1. Carelessness	(subtract 20 points)	_____
2. Inaccuracy	(subtract 20 points)	_____
3. Bias	(subtract 20 points)	_____
	FINAL SCORE:	_____

12. BRAZILIAN FILMMAKER: I saw several Brazilian officials, and a few American politicians and celebrities I had recognized from favorite movies. But the person who impressed me most at the ceremony, when I was one of only three students ever to receive an Esopus Film Award for documentary filmmaking, was my 93-year-old grandpa, who had flown in from Brazil to watch me receive this award for my self-produced documentary on an otherwise unknown indigenous community that is thriving along the Amazon River. Grandpa sat in the audience with an unimpressed, judgmental expression, but I couldn't miss the sparkle in his eye when they called my name.

		Points
1. Track Record	(out of 20 points)	_____
2. Suitable Program	(15 points)	_____
3. Contribution & Diversity	(15 points)	_____
4. Focus	(10 points)	_____
5. Prestige	(15 points)	_____
6. Legacy	(5 points)	_____
7. Special Qualities	(10 points)	_____
8. Character	(10 points)	_____
	TOTAL so far:	_____
Anything to subtract?		_____
1. Carelessness	(subtract 20 points)	_____
2. Inaccuracy	(subtract 20 points)	_____
3. Bias	(subtract 20 points)	_____
	FINAL SCORE:	_____

13. SEALS: On a university marine biology expedition off the coast of Maine, our scientist leader took us by motorboat to a spot with no land in sight. All seasoned swimmers, we were given snorkels and told to jump out of the motorboat—he had a surprise waiting there for us. I was fearful, but following his directions, I took the risk and dove in. Suddenly, 30 tremendous gray bodies—much larger than we were—swam toward us. When the huge seals arrived, they treated us as honored guests. They darted around playfully, and joyfully welcomed us into their world.

		Points
1. Track Record	(out of 20 points)	_____
2. Suitable Program	(15 points)	_____
3. Contribution & Diversity	(15 points)	_____
4. Focus	(10 points)	_____
5. Prestige	(15 points)	_____
6. Legacy	(5 points)	_____
7. Special Qualities	(10 points)	_____
8. Character	(10 points)	_____
	TOTAL so far:	_____
Anything to subtract?		_____
1. Carelessness	(subtract 20 points)	_____
2. Inaccuracy	(subtract 20 points)	_____
3. Bias	(subtract 20 points)	_____
	FINAL SCORE:	_____

14. DIVER: "Jump in!" my camp friends dared, as I looked down from the boulder at the water park. I was supposed to swing from a rope and plunge into the wave pool below. Lifeguards eyed me attentively. Posted signs warned that nonswimmers should not dive. I didn't really know how to swim, but I thought, "How dangerous could it be at a public water park?" So, responding to my friends' taunts, I took the risk and jumped in. Bad idea. I was drowning. I waved my arms frantically as I began to sink. A lifeguard jumped in and saved me. My friends were embarrassed; the lifeguard scolded me. I learned that some risks are best not taken.

		Points
1. Track Record	(out of 20 points)	_____
2. Suitable Program	(15 points)	_____
3. Contribution & Diversity	(15 points)	_____
4. Focus	(10 points)	_____
5. Prestige	(15 points)	_____
6. Legacy	(5 points)	_____
7. Special Qualities	(10 points)	_____
8. Character	(10 points)	_____
	TOTAL so far:	_____
Anything to subtract?		_____
1. Carelessness	(subtract 20 points)	_____
2. Inaccuracy	(subtract 20 points)	_____
3. Bias	(subtract 20 points)	_____
	FINAL SCORE:	_____

15. MINORITY MATHEMATICIAN: When I moved to the suburbs from New York City, I was the only black student in my school. I was also one of the only Asian Americans, since my father is African American and my mother is Sri Lankan. Kids called me "Tiger," in the tradition of Tiger Woods, and rudely assumed that I too played golf. Following Tiger's example, I worked hard in school, eager to show my classmates that minority students were capable of the highest academic achievements. Over the years, I've earned my A+ average taking all honors and AP courses. I'm the school's top math student, destroying stereotypes, one person at a time. I want to study Number Theory in college.

		Points
1. Track Record	(out of 20 points)	_____
2. Suitable Program	(15 points)	_____
3. Contribution & Diversity	(15 points)	_____
4. Focus	(10 points)	_____
5. Prestige	(15 points)	_____
6. Legacy	(5 points)	_____
7. Special Qualities	(10 points)	_____
8. Character	(10 points)	_____
	TOTAL so far:	_____
Anything to subtract?		_____
1. Carelessness	(subtract 20 points)	_____
2. Inaccuracy	(subtract 20 points)	_____
3. Bias	(subtract 20 points)	_____
	FINAL SCORE:	_____

16. RISK-FREE: I am fortunate enough to come from a family in which I have never had to face a risk or obstacle. I believe that careful planning and proper living almost guarantee a safe, risk-free setting in which children can grow up safe and secure. I have been privileged to live that life and am especially grateful to my parents for not exposing me to danger or obstacles. My dream is to become either an accountant or pharmacist—to establish a very stable career for myself with stable income, so that some day I might raise my own family in as good a setting as my parents have provided.

		Points
1. Track Record	(out of 20 points)	_____
2. Suitable Program	(15 points)	_____
3. Contribution & Diversity	(15 points)	_____
4. Focus	(10 points)	_____
5. Prestige	(15 points)	_____
6. Legacy	(5 points)	_____
7. Special Qualities	(10 points)	_____
8. Character	(10 points)	_____
	TOTAL so far:	_____
Anything to subtract?		_____
1. Carelessness	(subtract 20 points)	_____
2. Inaccuracy	(subtract 20 points)	_____
3. Bias	(subtract 20 points)	_____
	FINAL SCORE:	_____

17. SOLO SINGER: "Bravo!" people called from the audience, after the last note of my solo at the State Hall. I was terrified to perform in front of so many people, but I knew inside that the rewards were far greater than the risk, so I persevered. "Encore!" others screamed, much to my delight. I had prepared a little piece to perform—I had composed it myself. I wondered if this would make a suitable encore. I closed my eyes for a moment and took a deep breath, wondering if this is how all composers feel before a premiere. And I went for the challenge. I sang my little composition a cappella, and once again heard "Bravo!" at the end.

		Points
1. Track Record	(out of 20 points)	_____
2. Suitable Program	(15 points)	_____
3. Contribution & Diversity	(15 points)	_____
4. Focus	(10 points)	_____
5. Prestige	(15 points)	_____
6. Legacy	(5 points)	_____
7. Special Qualities	(10 points)	_____
8. Character	(10 points)	_____
	TOTAL so far:	_____
Anything to subtract?		_____
1. Carelessness	(subtract 20 points)	_____
2. Inaccuracy	(subtract 20 points)	_____
3. Bias	(subtract 20 points)	_____
	FINAL SCORE:	_____

18. INTERVIEWEE: Going for a college interview represented the first great risk for me. I had never interviewed for so much as a job or internship before, and here I was trying to make an impression that would influence the rest of my life. I did enormous preparation. I read up on the names of all the admissions officers and familiarized myself with their photos. I practiced in front of the mirror. On the day of the interview, I enjoyed it so much, that I wanted to become an admissions officer.

		Points
1. Track Record	(out of 20 points)	_____
2. Suitable Program	(15 points)	_____
3. Contribution & Diversity	(15 points)	_____
4. Focus	(10 points)	_____
5. Prestige	(15 points)	_____
6. Legacy	(5 points)	_____
7. Special Qualities	(10 points)	_____
8. Character	(10 points)	_____
	TOTAL so far:	_____
Anything to subtract?		_____
1. Carelessness	(subtract 20 points)	_____
2. Inaccuracy	(subtract 20 points)	_____
3. Bias	(subtract 20 points)	_____
	FINAL SCORE:	_____

19. BEGINNER SKIER: The day I took my first step on skis constituted an enormous risk for me. I had never done anything athletic before. My first loves were always sedentary activities like painting pictures, stamp collecting and chess. Here I was, looking down the bunny slope, wearing a parka and the latest equipment. The only problem was I didn't know how to ski and I was terrified. I saw an ambulance at the foot of the mountain. I saw a blind man whiz past me. Surely, I can do this, I told myself. My lesson began. An hour later, I was off the bunny slope and onto the real slope skiing.

		Points
1. Track Record	(out of 20 points)	_____
2. Suitable Program	(15 points)	_____
3. Contribution & Diversity	(15 points)	_____
4. Focus	(10 points)	_____
5. Prestige	(15 points)	_____
6. Legacy	(5 points)	_____
7. Special Qualities	(10 points)	_____
8. Character	(10 points)	_____
	TOTAL so far:	_____
Anything to subtract?		_____
1. Carelessness	(subtract 20 points)	_____
2. Inaccuracy	(subtract 20 points)	_____
3. Bias	(subtract 20 points)	_____
	FINAL SCORE:	_____

20. DIVORCE VICTIM: When my parents announced their divorce, I was adamant against getting help. Despite my drug use, I thought I was handling the crisis well. Seeing a psychiatrist represented too great a risk. "How could she solve my numerous problems?" I asked myself. But, appeasing my mother, I agreed to "interview" the doctor. She seemed fun—understanding me perfectly. Since then, I enjoy my weekly visits, and have become more able to deal with my problems. Best of all, I've stopped doing drugs.

		Points
1. Track Record	(out of 20 points)	_____
2. Suitable Program	(15 points)	_____
3. Contribution & Diversity	(15 points)	_____
4. Focus	(10 points)	_____
5. Prestige	(15 points)	_____
6. Legacy	(5 points)	_____
7. Special Qualities	(10 points)	_____
8. Character	(10 points)	_____
	TOTAL so far:	_____
Anything to subtract?		_____
1. Carelessness	(subtract 20 points)	_____
2. Inaccuracy	(subtract 20 points)	_____
3. Bias	(subtract 20 points)	_____
	FINAL SCORE:	_____

Interpreting Your Results

Although many will argue that the admissions process is very subjective (and they will be partly right) and that there are no "right" answers and no "wrong" answers, what I want you to see from this exercise is that certain essays win far more points than others—depending on the criteria. Look at the scores you've given to applicants. Based on your scores, list your top four candidates in order. Only two or three of them can be accepted into your college (representing 10 to 15 percent) if your college is among the *most competitive* colleges. Now determine Candidate #1 (definitely accepted if this is a most-competitive college or not-so-competitive college) and Candidate #2 (most likely to be accepted if this is a most-competitive college; definitely accepted at other colleges). Candidate #3 (definitely accepted if the college accept rate is at least 15 percent) is more likely to be accepted than Candidate #4 (only accepted if the college accept rate is at least 20 percent). A fifth candidate would only be accepted if the college admit rate is at least 25 percent.

YOUR CHOICES

If you were on the Admissions Committee for one of the most competitive colleges in the United States, you would be asked to select two students out of the 20 essays. The rest would be deferred or declined admission. Which two would you accept?

1. _____

2. _____

Who would be your third and fourth choice if you were on the committee at a school that admitted 15 percent or 20 percent?

3. _____

4. _____

Now compare your grading and selections to the author's answers to make sure you understand the overall concept of how essays are perceived. There may be some slight differences of interpretation. Don't worry about those. That's the subjectivity factor. And values may differ slightly from one college to another. The aim is to master the overall concept.

Answers

1. CLOTHESHORSE		Points	Explanation
1. Track Record	(out of 20 points)	0	
2. Suitable Program	(15 points)	0	
3. Contribution & Diversity	(15 points)	0	
4. Focus	(15 points)	0	
5. Prestige	(10 points)	0	
6. Legacy	(5 points)	0	
7. Special Qualities	(10 points)	0	
8. Character	(10 points)	0	
	TOTAL so far:	0	
Anything to subtract?			
1. Carelessness	(subtract 20 points)	____	
2. Inaccuracy	(subtract 20 points)	____	
3. Bias	(subtract 20 points)	____	
	FINAL SCORE:	0	

2. ASTRONOMER

		Points	Explanation
1. Track Record	(out of 20 points)	20	*Yes. 3 years' research plus patent*
2. Suitable Program	(15 points)	15	*Yes, assuming we offer Astronomy and Physics*
3. Contribution & Diversity	(15 points)	15	*At some colleges, women in Physics are relatively rare*
4. Focus	(10 points)	10	
5. Prestige	(15 points)	15	*Having a patent is prestigious*
6. Legacy	(5 points)	0	
7. Special Qualities	(10 points)	10	*Assuming we're in need of more Physics and Astronomy students*
8. Character	(10 points)	0	
	TOTAL so far:	85	

Anything to subtract?

1. Carelessness	(subtract 20 points)	_____	
2. Inaccuracy	(subtract 20 points)	_____	
3. Bias	(subtract 20 points)	_____	
	FINAL SCORE:	**85**	

3. BASEBALL JANE

		Points	Explanation
1. Track Record	(out of 20 points)	0	
2. Suitable Program	(15 points)	0	
3. Contribution & Diversity	(15 points)	15	*Although this doesn't fall into usual definitions of "Diversity," a girl playing on a boys' team could be viewed by some as "integrating" a team and contributing to diversity*
4. Focus	(10 points)	0	

5. Prestige	(15 points)	0
6. Legacy	(5 points)	0
7. Special Qualities	(10 points)	0
8. Character	(10 points)	0
	TOTAL so far:	15

Anything to subtract?

1. Carelessness	(subtract 20 points)	_____
2. Inaccuracy	(subtract 20 points)	_____
3. Bias	(subtract 20 points)	_____
	FINAL SCORE:	**15**

4. SURFER		Points	Explanation
1. Track Record	(out of 20 points)	20	*Although putting oneself in harm's way and pursuing one's own physical limits is NOT considered by all to be an optimal or even wise path to a career in physical therapy*
2. Suitable Program	(15 points)	15	*Yes, assuming we offer Physical Therapy*
3. Contribution & Diversity	(15 points)	0	
4. Focus	(10 points)	10	
5. Prestige	(15 points)	0	
6. Legacy	(5 points)	0	
7. Special Qualities	(10 points)	0	
8. Character	(10 points)	0	
	TOTAL so far:	45	

Anything to subtract?

1. Carelessness	(subtract 20 points)	_____
2. Inaccuracy	(subtract 20 points)	_____
3. Bias	(subtract 20 points)	_____

FINAL SCORE: 45

5. INDIAN ITINERARY		Points	Explanation
1. Track Record	(out of 20 points)	0	
2. Suitable Program	(15 points)	0	
3. Contribution & Diversity	(15 points)	15	*The applicant is Native American*
4. Focus	(10 points)	0	
5. Prestige	(15 points)	0	
6. Legacy	(5 points)	0	
7. Special Qualities	(10 points)	0	
8. Character	(10 points)	0	
	TOTAL so far:	15	

Anything to subtract?

1. Carelessness	(subtract 20 points)	_____
2. Inaccuracy	(subtract 20 points)	_____
3. Bias	(subtract 20 points)	_____

FINAL SCORE: 15

6. MESSY ARTIST		Points	Explanation
1. Track Record	(out of 20 points)	20	
2. Suitable Program	(15 points)	15	*Yes, assuming we offer Studio Art*

3. Contribution & Diversity	(15 points)	0
4. Focus	(10 points)	10
5. Prestige	(15 points)	0
6. Legacy	(5 points)	0
7. Special Qualities	(10 points)	0
8. Character	(10 points)	0
	TOTAL so far:	45

Anything to subtract?

1. Carelessness	(subtract 20 points)	____	
2. Inaccuracy	(subtract 20 points)	____	
3. Bias	(subtract 20 points)	0	*Although her comment about the sloppiness of "a typical college student" borders on bias*
	FINAL SCORE:	**45**	

7. GROUNDSKEEPER		Points	Explanation
1. Track Record	(out of 20 points)	0	
2. Suitable Program	(15 points)	0	
3. Contribution & Diversity	(15 points)	0	
4. Focus	(10 points)	0	
5. Prestige	(15 points)	0	
6. Legacy	(5 points)	0	
7. Special Qualities	(10 points)	0	
8. Character	(10 points)	10	*Not everyone would consider the student's willingness to put up with boredom (after the resort went back on its promise to let the volunteer use the resort's facilities)*

a sign of strong character. But for those who would argue that the applicant showed character by staying on the job despite his boredom, we'll award 10 points.

TOTAL so far: 10

Anything to subtract?

1. Carelessness	(subtract 20 points)	−20	*Far too many spelling errors*
2. Inaccuracy	(subtract 20 points)	____	
3. Bias	(subtract 20 points)	____	
	FINAL SCORE:	**−10**	

8. FRENCH ENTHUSIAST		Points	Explanation
1. Track Record	(out of 20 points)	5	*Although this student demonstrates some minimal track record with the French language, the track record is hardly impressive. The student scored a mediocre 500 on the SAT II, and is proud of it, and doesn't really show any depth of knowledge about France. So we'll only give partial credit.*
2. Suitable Program	(15 points)	15	
3. Contribution & Diversity	(15 points)	0	
4. Focus	(10 points)	10	
5. Prestige	(15 points)	0	
6. Legacy	(5 points)	0	
7. Special Qualities	(10 points)	0	
8. Character	(10 points)	0	
	TOTAL so far:	30	

Anything to subtract?

1. Carelessness	(subtract 20 points)	_____
2. Inaccuracy	(subtract 20 points)	_____
3. Bias	(subtract 20 points)	_____
	FINAL SCORE:	**30**

9. THUNDERSTORM		Points	Explanation
1. Track Record	(out of 20 points)	20	
2. Suitable Program	(15 points)	15	*Yes, assuming we offer Meteorology*
3. Contribution & Diversity	(15 points)	0	
4. Focus	(10 points)	10	
5. Prestige	(15 points)	0	
6. Legacy	(5 points)	0	
7. Special Qualities	(10 points)	10	*Assuming we need more Meteorology majors at our college*
8. Character	(10 points)	0	
	TOTAL so far:	55	

Anything to subtract?

1. Carelessness	(subtract 20 points)	_____
2. Inaccuracy	(subtract 20 points)	_____
3. Bias	(subtract 20 points)	_____
	FINAL SCORE:	**55**

10. HOMESICK		Points	Explanation
1. Track Record	(out of 20 points)	0	
2. Suitable Program	(15 points)	0	

3. Contribution & Diversity   (15 points)   0

4. Focus   (10 points)   0

5. Prestige   (15 points)   0

6. Legacy   (5 points)   0

7. Special Qualities   (10 points)   0

8. Character   (10 points)   0

                              TOTAL so far: 0

Anything to subtract?

1. Carelessness   (subtract 20 points) _____

2. Inaccuracy   (subtract 20 points) _____

3. Bias   (subtract 20 points) _____

                              FINAL SCORE: 0

11. ISRAEL ITINERARY		Points	Explanation
1. Track Record	(out of 20 points)	0	
2. Suitable Program	(15 points)	0	
3. Contribution & Diversity	(15 points)	0	
4. Focus	(10 points)	0	
5. Prestige	(15 points)	0	
6. Legacy	(5 points)	0	
7. Special Qualities	(10 points)	0	
8. Character	(10 points)	0	
	TOTAL so far:	0	

Anything to subtract?

1. Carelessness   (subtract 20 points) _____

2. Inaccuracy   (subtract 20 points) _____

| 3. Bias | (subtract 20 points) | 0 | *Although, the flippancy of describing a major historic site like Masada as "where ancient Jews committed suicide" could easily be considered bias or at least lack of cultural respect* |
| | **FINAL SCORE:** | **0** | |

12. BRAZILIAN FILMMAKER		Points	Explanation
1. Track Record	(out of 20 points)	20	
2. Suitable Program	(15 points)	15	*Assuming we offer Anthropology, Documentary Filmmaking, or Journalism*
3. Contribution & Diversity	(15 points)	15	*Grandparent from Brazil*
4. Focus	(10 points)	10	
5. Prestige	(15 points)	15	*As winner of a national film contest*
6. Legacy	(5 points)	0	
7. Special Qualities	(10 points)	0	
8. Character	(10 points)	0	
	TOTAL so far:	75	
Anything to subtract?			
1. Carelessness	(subtract 20 points)	_____	
2. Inaccuracy	(subtract 20 points)	_____	
3. Bias	(subtract 20 points)	_____	
	FINAL SCORE:	**75**	

13. SEALS		Points	Explanation
1. Track Record	(out of 20 points)	20	
2. Suitable Program	(15 points)	15	*Assuming we offer Marine Biology*

3. Contribution & Diversity	(15 points)	0
4. Focus	(10 points)	10
5. Prestige	(15 points)	0
6. Legacy	(5 points)	0
7. Special Qualities	(10 points)	0
8. Character	(10 points)	0
	TOTAL so far:	45

Anything to subtract?

1. Carelessness	(subtract 20 points)	____
2. Inaccuracy	(subtract 20 points)	____
3. Bias	(subtract 20 points)	____
	FINAL SCORE:	**45**

14. DIVER		Points	Explanation
1. Track Record	(out of 20 points)	0	
2. Suitable Program	(15 points)	0	
3. Contribution & Diversity	(15 points)	0	
4. Focus	(10 points)	0	
5. Prestige	(15 points)	0	
6. Legacy	(5 points)	0	
7. Special Qualities	(10 points)	0	
8. Character	(10 points)	0	
	TOTAL so far:	0	

Anything to subtract?

| 1. Carelessness | (subtract 20 points) | ____ |
| 2. Inaccuracy | (subtract 20 points) | ____ |

| 3. Bias | (subtract 20 points) ____ |
| **FINAL SCORE:** | **0** |

15. MINORITY MATHEMATICIAN	Points	Explanation
1. Track Record	(out of 20 points)	20	
2. Suitable Program	(15 points)	15	*Math, Number Theory*
3. Contribution & Diversity	(15 points)	15	
4. Focus	(10 points)	10	
5. Prestige	(15 points)	0	
6. Legacy	(5 points)	0	
7. Special Qualities	(10 points)	0	
8. Character	(10 points)	10	
	TOTAL so far:	70	

Anything to subtract?

1. Carelessness	(subtract 20 points) ____
2. Inaccuracy	(subtract 20 points) ____
3. Bias	(subtract 20 points) ____
FINAL SCORE:	**70**

16. RISK-FREE	Points	Explanation
1. Track Record	(out of 20 points)	0	
2. Suitable Program	(15 points)	0	
3. Contribution & Diversity	(15 points)	0	
4. Focus	(10 points)	0	
5. Prestige	(15 points)	0	

6. Legacy	(5 points)	0
7. Special Qualities	(10 points)	0
8. Character	(10 points)	0
	TOTAL so far:	0

Anything to subtract?

1. Carelessness	(subtract 20 points)	_____
2. Inaccuracy	(subtract 20 points)	_____
3. Bias	(subtract 20 points)	_____
	FINAL SCORE:	**0**

17. SOLO SINGER		Points	Explanation
1. Track Record	(out of 20 points)	20	
2. Suitable Program	(15 points)	15	*Assuming we offer composition*
3. Contribution & Diversity	(15 points)	0	
4. Focus	(10 points)	10	
5. Prestige	(15 points)	15	*A successful musical composer could add prestige*
6. Legacy	(5 points)	0	
7. Special Qualities	(10 points)	0	
8. Character	(10 points)	0	
	TOTAL so far:	60	

Anything to subtract?

1. Carelessness	(subtract 20 points)	_____
2. Inaccuracy	(subtract 20 points)	_____
3. Bias	(subtract 20 points)	_____
	FINAL SCORE:	**60**

18. INTERVIEWEE		Points	Explanation
1. Track Record	(out of 20 points)	0	
2. Suitable Program	(15 points)	0	
3. Contribution & Diversity	(15 points)	0	
4. Focus	(10 points)	10	
5. Prestige	(15 points)	0	
6. Legacy	(5 points)	0	
7. Special Qualities	(10 points)	0	
8. Character	(10 points)	0	
	TOTAL so far:	10	

Anything to subtract?

1. Carelessness	(subtract 20 points)	_____	
2. Inaccuracy	(subtract 20 points)	_____	
3. Bias	(subtract 20 points)	_____	
	FINAL SCORE:	**10**	

19. BEGINNER SKIER		Points	Explanation
1. Track Record	(out of 20 points)	0	
2. Suitable Program	(15 points)	0	
3. Contribution & Diversity	(15 points)	0	
4. Focus	(10 points)	0	
5. Prestige	(15 points)	0	
6. Legacy	(5 points)	0	
7. Special Qualities	(10 points)	0	
8. Character	(10 points)	0	
	TOTAL so far:	0	

Anything to subtract?

1. Carelessness	(subtract 20 points)	____
2. Inaccuracy	(subtract 20 points)	____
3. Bias	(subtract 20 points)	____
	FINAL SCORE:	**0**

20. DIVORCE VICTIM		Points	Explanation
1. Track Record	(out of 20 points)	0	
2. Suitable Program	(15 points)	0	
3. Contribution & Diversity	(15 points)	0	
4. Focus	(10 points)	0	
5. Prestige	(15 points)	0	
6. Legacy	(5 points)	0	
7. Special Qualities	(10 points)	0	
8. Character	(10 points)	0	
	TOTAL so far:	0	

Anything to subtract?

1. Carelessness	(subtract 20 points)	____
2. Inaccuracy	(subtract 20 points)	____
3. Bias	(subtract 20 points)	____
	FINAL SCORE:	**0**

Who Gets Accepted?

So now that you've read all the essays and compared answers, who got accepted? Most likely you agreed that the Astronomer (score 85), who holds a patent, should be accepted as the first pick. The Brazilian Filmmaker (75) was also very impressive, as was the Minority Mathematician (70). Next in line, if the admit rate is higher than 15 percent, is the Solo Singer (60), followed by Thunderstorm (55). Notice that the supposed economic backgrounds and ethnic backgrounds vary among these applicants, as do the interests and activities each pursued. Note that there is no singular formula that gets you admitted, but the most appealing candidates are clearly the ones who have been working hard in school and have invested themselves into the activities that interest them the most. Some of these activities (science and math, for example) are clearly valued more than others (clothes shopping, amusement parks, etc.) by colleges.

Also observe that some perfectly wonderful candidates ultimately are turned away. When you write your own essays, it will be important to keep the criteria in mind (and the scorecard in hand), to make sure you earn as many points as possible.

Once you understand the general scoring system (which I'll emphasize again, differs at each college, but reflects the same general values), it's time for you to decide which messages you want your essay to communicate to the Admissions Committee. The next chapter focuses on making sure that your essay highlights your best qualities.

Your Message
(15 Minutes)

What Your Essay Must Say

If you had 20 seconds in the elevator with the Head of Admissions of your dream college, and he/she suddenly asked you, "Why should we take you out of all the thousands of kids applying here?" how would you answer the question? Jot down your answer. This answer will come in handy—especially in the fourth paragraph of your essay (you'll see why later)—when you're writing your essay, and also when you go for interviews. In fact, your answer should supply the theme of your entire application. When you're filling out your application, you should keep this answer in front of you the whole time.

Write your initial answer here:

"Take me because I will be the only applicant (or one of the only applicants) who will have _____
_____."

Your answer should consist of something you are most proud of—or something the people around you (your teachers, your parents, your school) would say that you *should* be most proud of. Of course, this will depend on your values and theirs. But in all cases, the credential that you choose—the reason colleges should accept you—should be something that somehow contributes productively to your immediate family, community, society, or to making the world a better place.

"But I don't have any one single credential that makes me outstanding," students often say. In that case, I recommend that you think of your three best credentials (related or unrelated), and combine them into a single sentence.

Example 1: "I am the only applicant who is captain of the Central High School Water Polo Team who also has volunteered more than 150 hours in the Children's Ward at Central Valley Hospital, and who has won the Junior History Award at Central High."

Example 2: "I am the only applicant who has read all the novels of Leo Tolstoy and Dostoyevsky, studied Russian in high school through Level 3, and led my school's battery recycling program."

Example 3: "I am the only applicant who is a school newspaper cartoonist, who takes advanced drawing classes at the Central Valley Art Academy after school, and who painted a portrait that is permanently displayed in the school's main office."

Are you unsure about which credentials might be impressive to colleges? Here are some outstanding options to give you a sense of which accomplishments are impressive: An award you won, a fund-raiser you led, a work of art you created, an audition you passed, a difficult piece you performed, a public speech you gave, a good deed you performed, a good trend you started, something you invented, research you conducted, an original discovery you made, a publication, a patent, a lesson you taught, an experience you survived, a business you started, a local problem you helped solve, an unusual interest in which you're an expert, an idea you've been exploring and want to explore further, winning a difficult election, preventing a crime, saving the day, rescuing someone (or his/her cat or dog), volunteering when nobody else would, solving a difficult puzzle, taking an actual college course, helping a needy person in a special way, breaking down social barriers, working to help support your family, striving to meet an athletic goal, having your work critiqued by a famous authority, or enabling a cultural exchange.

Note that most of the above suggestions do not require money, exotic travel, costly summer programs, or other major expenses. You don't have to be rich to have had worthwhile experiences that interest even the most competitive colleges.

Avoid the following answers:

1. "Take me because I got my driver's license and I'm frequently the designated driver."

   (This would give the impression that you're just another stereotypical bimbo, car-obsessed, cookie-cutter teenager—boring and not the kind of kid admissions officers seek.)

2. "I'm a really nice, respectful, all-around good student, but I haven't done anything special or won any major prizes."

   (This too will work against you, making you sound dull, and not providing any positive reason to accept you.)

3. "I'm a good kid. I drink responsibly, and I don't do drugs."

   (This says what you don't *do, rather than what wonderful deeds you* do *do. And it implies that you're surrounded by underage drinkers.)*

4. "I'm very popular and a real leader, and I've heard that colleges want leaders."

(Popularity is not valued by college admissions officers in general. Leadership is. But you need to specify what worthwhile cause you've actually led to make this answer helpful. A recycling campaign? A chamber-group practice? A fund-raiser?)

5. "My politics are very liberal, and I've heard you prefer liberal students."

(The colleges reputed to be the most liberal pride themselves on not accepting students based on political perspectives.)

6. "I have a lot of school spirit, and I'm a big Dreamers fan! Go Dreamers!"

(Colleges don't accept students based on applicants knowing the school cheer or claiming to support the school team. They know that if you're accepted into a different college, you'll quickly master that school's cheer just as readily.)

Now list two or three more of your best credentials (in addition to the one you listed above) that you would want to tell an Admissions Dean:

1. _____

2. _____

3. _____

Keep this list handy. You will want to insert these items into your essay somewhere—to make sure to tell the admissions staff. In the "experience essay" (Common App Essay Choice 1), I generally recommend that students insert these "talking points" into the fourth paragraph (out of five paragraphs). But we'll discuss structure more in Chapter 5.

• 10-MINUTE BREAK •

Now It's Time to Pick a Topic
(30 Minutes, Including Daydreaming)

Finally you get to choose a topic! Here is some advice:

The strongest essays answer Option 1 on the Common Application: "*Evaluate a significant experience, achievement, risk you have taken, or ethical dilemma you have faced and its impact on you.*"

Do You Prefer a Different Topic?

If you would prefer to focus your essay on Option 2 instead ("*Discuss some issue . . .*") jump to Chapter 9, where that essay is discussed. If you would prefer to address Option 3 or 4 ("Describe a person, character or art work . . ."), jump to Chapter 10. And if you would prefer Option 5 ("an experience that illustrates what you would bring to the diversity" of colleges), read this chapter, plus Chapter 7.

TIP 1: If you're going to stick with Essay Prompt Option 1, base your essay on one of the first three parts of the essay prompt (not the "ethical dilemma"): Either write about a significant experience, achievement, or risk you have taken—choose one of the three—and its impact on you. Avoid the "ethical dilemma" as a topic, since there are so many pitfalls to writing about ethics in a college application essay, and your sense of ethics compared to some admissions officers' may be very different. For example, if you see another student cheating, many colleges would advocate "reporting" that violation, but some colleges would call that kind of reporting "tattling," and find it unethical to tattle. I have never seen a great response to the ethical dilemma prompt. Don't try to be the first. You don't want to go there.

TIP 2: If you choose the "risk" option, make sure it's not a risk that admissions officers would consider foolhardy or that deliberately places you in harm's way. Sample foolhardy risks include: skydiving, bungee jumping, swimming with sharks, driving without a license, challenging someone to a fistfight, diving into the pool without knowing how to swim, etc. Applicants who come across as potential liabilities are not attractive to admissions officers.

TIP 3: Avoid writing about risks that make you look bad (e.g., getting lost in a shopping mall, getting beaten up, getting sued) and also risks that don't sound risky enough and make you sound wimpy (giving an oral presentation before your class, starting piano lessons, making new friends, having a tooth filled) or spoiled (e.g., complaining about being the only kid at the junior prom who arrived without a limo, the only kid on the teen tour without designer luggage, having to sit next to a stranger on the airplane ride to the exotic resort). There are plenty of good risks (e.g., auditioning, running for office, attempting to create a work of art/music, speaking at a rally, attempting to communicate in another language, designing an innovative fund-raiser, volunteering for a difficult community service project, etc.).

TIP 4: The best essays generally focus on only one episode in the applicant's life. Don't worry that you're leaving out other revealing episodes. The episode you choose will tell volumes about you. Never try to summarize your résumé, biography, chronology, or credentials in 500 words.

TIP 5: Don't worry about how you're going to go about inserting your "true personality." Every story you tell will inherently reveal to the reader all about you. You'd be surprised.

Why should we accept YOU?

That's the question that colleges want you to answer on your application. Don't lose sight of that question.

Time to Choose Your Topic

STEP 1: For your first-choice college, go to the college's website, and look at Academics and then Majors or Departments. Select the major that you think is best suited to the experiences you have had so far. (Yes, most colleges insist that you don't have to select your major in advance, but play along for now. If you can't decide between two majors that you love equally and in which you have a track record already, choose the one that you think most people won't choose; your odds will be better much of the time.)

Write the major here: _____.

Make sure you write the name of the major exactly as the college writes it if you are targeting the essay for a specific college. If the college calls the subject Biological Sciences, instead of Biology, then you too should call it Biological Sciences in your application. Likewise, if the college calls the subject Life Sciences (with an "s" at the end), Life Science (without the "s"), General Biology, or Bioengineering, make sure you refer to the subject the same way. If you're writing the essay for the Common Application and you know that several colleges will be reading the same version of the essay, then you may refer to the major by the generic name, using lowercase letters: biology or biological sciences (e.g., "I'm hoping to pursue biological sciences in college.").

STEP 2: Make a list of your five best (unique) reasons, credentials, or accomplishments for that major. (If you can't think of any credentials that you have that demonstrate why that major suits you, then go back and find a more suitable major.) See if any of your four top credentials (the ones you listed in Chapter 3) point to one of the majors offered by Dreamschool.

Only use recent (high-school-age) credentials—nothing from elementary school days or even middle school days, unless it's a national- or international-level credential. Sample national- or international-level credentials: Having a speaking role in a Hollywood film, performing an instrumental solo at Carnegie Hall, competing as a gymnast in the International Olympics, winning the National Spelling Bee, writing an article that's published in a national publication (*The New York Times, Time* magazine, etc.), having your artwork exhibited at a nationally known museum, dancing in *The Nutcracker* with a professional ballet company, soloing with a major opera company, starring on Broadway, earning a patent for an original invention, saving a life, raising an inordinate amount of money for a major charity ($10,000+). Nobody on the Admissions Committee wants to read essays about how you were the first to learn to read in nursery school, or how cute you looked when you won the starring role at age five in the ballet school performance.

LIST YOUR REASONS, CREDENTIALS, AND RELATED ACCOMPLISHMENTS HERE:

1. _____

2. _____

3. _____

4. _____

5. _____

SAMPLE: John Doe wants to apply to be a Peace Studies major at Random University.

JOHN DOE'S 5 MOST RELATED CREDENTIALS

1. John took a summer course in Conflict Resolution at nearby Commonpoint College.

2. John chaired the Student Conflict Resolution Committee at high school.

3. John was an excellent student in his American History class.

4. John worked in a supermarket after school, and won the Employee of the Month award for helping to keep the peace.

5. John took part in a reenactment of the Battle of Gettysburg.

SAMPLE: Jane Smith wants to be a Sports Management major at Random University.

JANE SMITH'S 5 MOST RELATED CREDENTIALS

1. Jane is the captain of the girls' soccer team in her high school.

2. Jane volunteers regularly to coach a soccer team of elementary-school girls.

3. Jane organized a fund-raiser to buy new field goals for her school.

4. Jane worked as an intern at a local tennis club.

5. Jane took a summer course on Finance at nearby Commonpoint College.

STEP 3: Using the major that you've listed and each of the five credentials that you've listed, think of the personal stories and anecdotes that you associate with each of those five credentials. Make a list of five possible interesting true stories from your life—one for each credential that you've listed—that illustrate your interest or skill in that major. Along with each story subject, jot down some of the skills, abilities, or talents that your story would illustrate.

Story 1: _____

  Skills illustrated: _____

  _____

Story 2: _____

  Skills illustrated: _____

  _____

Story 3: _____

    Skills illustrated: _____

    _____

Story 4: _____

    Skills illustrated: _____

    _____

Story 5: _____

    Skills illustrated: _____

    _____

SAMPLE FOR JOHN DOE (BASED ON THE FIVE CREDENTIALS HE LISTED):

1. How John resolved a simulated conflict in his Conflict Resolution summer course.

   (Skills illustrated: negotiation, initiative, interest in peace making)

2. The crisis on the Student Conflict Resolution Committee and John's proposed solution.

   (Skills illustrated: negotiation, leadership)

3. How John interviewed a World War II veteran in researching and writing a paper for his American History class.

   (Skills and interest illustrated: interviewing, research, initiative, history passion)

4. The time that a fight broke out in the supermarket and John resolved it peacefully.

   (Skills illustrated: negotiation, leadership, initiative)

5. Rehearsing for the Gettysburg reenactment.

(Skills and interest illustrated: initiative, history passion, imagination, collaboration)

SAMPLE FOR JANE SMITH (BASED ON THE FIVE CREDENTIALS SHE LISTED):

1. The day the older soccer team captain was hospitalized and Jane was asked to take over.

(Skills illustrated: leadership, responsiveness, reliability)

2. The time two fathers went out of control at the girls' soccer game she was coaching, and Jane stepped in.

(Skills illustrated: leadership, negotiation, resolve, courage)

3. How Jane created a most original fund-raiser that brought in $5,000 to purchase new field goals for school soccer.

(Skills and interests illustrated: initiative, fund-raising, creativity, sports passion)

4. The day the famous tennis pro came to the club to practice—and no courts were free.

(Skills illustrated: leadership, decision making, negotiation, fairness)

5. When the major corporation CFO guest-lectured in Jane's Finance class—and gave Jane his personal advice.

(Skills illustrated: initiative, interviewing, resourcefulness)

TIP 6: You might have noticed that essay topics are a lot easier to find if you have had interesting real-world interactions. But you don't have to go to foreign countries, fancy resorts, or expensive summer camps to have these interactions. You don't even have to travel within the United States.

Most of the best essays—with the best real-world interactions—emerge from volunteering, internships, research, jobs, or creating an original work. In other words, engaging stories about something *positive* you've actively done, accomplished, or experienced, and being able to tell the reader how you did what you did. That's what makes the strongest essays.

STEP 4: From the five episodes (anecdotes and stories) that you've listed, choose the one that you enjoy telling most, and the one that presents you in the best light. Most likely both will point to the same essay topic. That's your essay topic. Write it here:

Essay topic: _____

Skills illustrated: _____

STEP 5: Keep the remaining four topics handy. You will probably want to refer to them in the fourth paragraph of your essay where you mention your other related credentials. But you'll find out more about this in the next chapter.

ALTERNATIVE APPROACH

(Skip this section if you already have your topic.)

(What if you have no idea what you want to study or have no credentials?)

While it's usually better to have some idea of what you'd like to study, not everyone does. And not everybody arrives at senior year with a solid list of appealing credentials. You can still write a strong essay, even if you have no clue as to what your dream major might be. But you'll need to think of the five achievements of which you are most proud. If you didn't win any awards, you might list some different ways in which you've helped people (for example, volunteering as a tutor, or working at a job after school to help the family meet its budget, or farm chores, or singing in the church choir, or helping to organize a food drive, or shoveling a neighbor's snow, or pet sitting).

TO START: Make a list of five of your best credentials, talents, or achievements that you want to be sure to tell the admissions office—before you even look at the essay question. If you have trouble coming up with five items, ask your family members to help you think of five of your best qualities, achievements, or credentials.

The five qualities should not be adjectives. In other words, you don't want to list:

1. I'm sociable

2. I'm thoughtful

3. I'm creative

4. I'm responsible

5. I'm athletic

Instead, the five qualities should tell the admissions officers about the greatest things you *did* or *accomplished* in the last four or so years.

SAMPLE ACCOMPLISHMENTS:

1. I helped organize a fund-raising fashion show at school to raise money for a neighborhood boy who had cancer, and we managed to collect $1,200.

2. Every weekend I visit the senior citizen home nearby to spend time with some of the residents who don't get any other visitors.

3. My painting from art class was exhibited at the local library.

4. At the local bookstore where I work after school, I was given a certificate from the manager for being the only one to show up during the blizzard.

5. As a result of my archery record, I was named captain of the varsity team.

LIST YOUR FIVE CREDENTIALS HERE:

Credential 1: _____

Credential 2: _____

Credential 3: _____

Credential 4: _____

Credential 5: _____

NEXT STEP: Using each of the five credentials that you've listed, think of the personal stories and anecdotes that you associate with those five credentials. Make a list here:

Story 1: _____

Story 2: _____

Story 3: _____

Story 4: _____

Story 5: _____

SAMPLE STORIES *(based on the sample accomplishments listed above):*

1. At the fund-raising fashion show, the principal got on stage to announce that this was the most thoughtful school event ever, and that a record amount of money was raised.

2. At the senior home, one of the residents told me how he escaped from a concentration camp during World War II, and I developed an interest in wartime history.

3. Try to draw a pineapple. That was the assignment the teacher gave when my painting was ultimately selected for the local library exhibit.

4. How I got to work the day of the blizzard.

5. The day the famous Olympic archer came to my archery class and offered me some personal tips on improving my aim.

NEXT STEP: From the five episodes (anecdotes and stories) that you've listed, choose the one that you enjoy telling most—or the one that presents you in the best light. Most likely both will point to the same essay topic. That's your essay topic. Write it here:

_____

Once you have your essay topic, you're almost ready to start writing. Believe it or not, finding the essay topic is usually considered the hardest part of the application process. So congratulations for having completed the hardest task of the whole application!

• **1 0 - M I N U T E B R E A K** •

The Structure of Your Essay
(2 Hours, Including Writing Your Essay)

Are you ready to write? First let's review what you're writing about, to make sure that you're clear.

Use the major, topic, and overall anecdote or story related to that topic that you selected during Chapter 4. Write that major, topic, and story here, so you remember what your essay is to be about.

1. Prospective first-choice major (if you know it):

_____

2. Related topic of essay: _____

3. Specific story: _____

I have found that some of the most engaging college application essays use the following, easy, one-page, 500-word format to answer the Common Application "experience" essay prompt. (No, this doesn't produce canned essays.)

Your Essay

FIRST PARAGRAPH: Open your essay like a novel (first or third person—
   your choice)
SECOND PARAGRAPH: Who, what, when, where, why, how
THIRD PARAGRAPH: Continue telling the story
FOURTH PARAGRAPH: Your credentials
FIFTH PARAGRAPH: Upbeat ending

Here is a sample of how to structure the entire essay:

1. Choice of major: Food science

2. Topic: Working at the bakery

3. Specific story: The time the famous food critic Julianna
   Brioche came to the bakery

FIRST PARAGRAPH: The first sentence should start like an action
novel, a play on the senses (taste, smell, sound, vision, touch),
or movie dialogue, using the most dramatic or intense aspects
of the story to captivate the reader—in case the admissions officer doesn't bother reading the second line. The rest of the first
paragraph should continue this way too. In the first paragraph,
use either first or third person—your choice.

Sample first paragraph (told like the beginning of a novel that plays on the senses):
   The dark chocolate was deep brown and bubbling in the pot, oozing as
   it melted and surrounded the white streaks of newly added milk. A
   heavy wooden spoon churned slowly through the mixture, helping the
   smooth liquid chocolate to thicken gradually. The aroma brought salivat-
   ing dessert lovers to the counter to steal extra whiffs of this most luxuri-
   ous smell and to beg for a taste of the batter.

SECOND PARAGRAPH: Now that you've captured the attention of the reader, the second paragraph should fill in the details of where you were, when this happened, how you found yourself in this situation.

Sample second paragraph (the who, what, when, where, why, how): That's how the brownies were being prepared for the visit of the famous food critic Julianna Brioche, who came to the bakery where I worked on Main Street in Centerville one wintry day last February. The bakery's owner had warned us that Ms. Brioche was an avid chocolate aficionado—and that the brownies that day had to be perfect—that the reputation of the bakery depended on it. And so, following the baker's favorite recipe as customers looked on, I set out to prepare the best brownies I had ever made.

THIRD PARAGRAPH: The third paragraph should simply continue telling the story.

Sample third paragraph: As the storefront became toasty, the bakery owner opened the front door, to let some of the heat escape, but that also let out the aroma of fresh-baking brownies, and the little shop began to crowd with eager customers. That's when Ms. Brioche made her grand entrance—amid the clamoring. And she ordered a plate of two brownies—one with walnuts and one without. She asked if we would serve them to her à la mode with vanilla ice cream. I tried to act casual, as if her appearance was an everyday event. Meanwhile customers who recognized her crowded around her table, waiting to hear her verdict. She seemed to like the attention.

FOURTH PARAGRAPH: This is the most important paragraph in the essay. Here is where you should throw in every last credential you want the admissions officers to know about you in relation to your chosen major. Remember that "elevator speech" from Chapter 3 where you had 20 seconds to tell an admissions officer your best credentials? *This paragraph* is *that elevator speech.* This paragraph *is* your 20 seconds alone with the admissions officer. This is also the paragraph where you might throw in abbreviated versions of the stories you were considering as essay alternatives in the previous chapter. (Remember you were asked to list five possible anecdotes or stories, and you chose only one to be your main essay. Well, now is the time to mention some of the other four, if it fits in well here.) This is the paragraph that really tells them your capabilities, your values, and what you've accomplished that makes you worthy of their college.

Sample fourth paragraph: This wasn't the first time I had to prove myself by baking. There was the time when I entered the Central County Bake-Off Competition and ended up winning First Place Baker at the County Fair—amid some rough competition including many professional bakers and bakery owners. And as a weekly volunteer in the kitchen of Central Hospital, I once baked a huge Portuguese farm bread for the patients, and the long-term-care patients have been raving about that loaf to this day. And then there was the time when I organized a bake sale at the Central Valley Shopping Mall to raise money for a local soup kitchen and regional food distribution center. Working with three other friends, we managed to raise $3,000 in one day, so we showed up again the following week and raised $4,000 more, a significant contribution to feed the hungry.

FIFTH PARAGRAPH: The fifth paragraph should wrap up the story by showing how these stories—especially the main essay topic— apply to your chosen (prospective) major. And this paragraph should also have an upbeat ending—a punchline.

Sample fifth paragraph: Back at the bakery, I was learning the power of food. Neighbors crowded in to chat and eat brownies, and I got to see firsthand how much of an impact an appealing recipe and a well-prepared treat can have on an otherwise too-busy-to-chat city neighborhood. I love the way food brings people together, and I would be thrilled to learn more about Food Science—beyond the instant gratification of baking—at Dreamschool College. In fact, seeing how people respond to simple brownies—both in the bakery and at the mall fund-raiser—made me more eager than ever to study international food distribution and ways to feed the hungry on a global basis. Oh, and in case you're wondering, Julianna Brioche said these were the best brownies she had ever tasted and gave the bakery her top five-star review.

As you can see, the essay tells a nice feel-good story. The reader can't help but like the applicant. We learn a lot about the applicant's values, although she never says, "I feel," or "I believe." We also get a sense that the reader has lots of food-related credentials and that she'd make an excellent Food Science major at our college.

ANOTHER SAMPLE ESSAY

1. Choice of major: Criminal Justice

2. Topic: Working at the City Morgue as a Photography Intern

3. Specific story: My first day at the internship

Sample first paragraph (drawing the reader in): The nude woman seemed to stare at me, and I felt like I was violating her privacy as I reached over to photograph the gash on her face. I had never met her when she was alive, but I knew there were many things she would have wanted to tell me about how she died. For starters, I could see clearly that she'd been hit quite hard. I wanted to make sure to document her multiple wounds, because I realized that my camera was one of the only voices that this woman had left to advocate for her. So I took a series of photos of her face from multiple angles.

Sample second paragraph (providing the who, what, when, where, why, how): That woman's body was the first of more than 20 bodies I photographed last summer, when I took on a photography internship at the City Medical Examiner's Office. My job was to help establish the facts of murders and deaths. And most of my photos were ultimately used as evidence in courtrooms. Because I was under age 18, I was not allowed to touch any of the bodies or move them, but I was able to photograph them just the same. So I worked five days a week, photographing and developing photos that captured the darker side of Central City.

Sample third paragraph (continuing the story): On one of the days, I photographed a man's body that had been punctured with bullet holes. Most of the bullets had been removed and taken to a separate lab for expert analysis. But I was asked to photograph all of the entryways for the bullets: there were eight. On another day, I was asked to photograph a man's body that had taken a great fall down a double flight of stairs. And another time, I photographed two adults who had been crushed in a car accident due to a drunk driver. On different occasions my job included meeting with detectives and police, and even showing up in court occasionally to see my photos being introduced into evidence.

Sample fourth paragraph (packing in the credentials; this is the paragraph where you can potentially pick up the most points and give the admissions officers good substantial reasons to want you): My job at the Medical Examiner's Office wasn't the first time I had been exposed to the criminal justice system. In the summer before my junior year of high school, I worked very closely with local law enforcement officials as a volunteer at the Harmony Shelter for Battered Women and Children. There, I mainly helped care for the children, so the mothers could tend to other chores. For my work I was ultimately given a Central City Community Service Award by Central City Mayor John Jones at a City Hall ceremony. I have also taken a course in my high school to earn certification as an Emergency Medical Technician and earned my Red Cross Lifeguard Certification as well—both important credentials to help protect my community. And this year at school I have been working with local drug enforcement officials as the president of my school's Students Against Drugs and Illegal Substances.

Sample fifth paragraph (wrap-up of original story, with a tie-in to academics):
Back at the Medical Examiner's Office, the photo I took of the dead woman on my first day of the internship proved very helpful in court. The result was that a dangerous gang of four that had been threatening the city for two years was finally convicted. Being able to help Central City stand up to violent criminals and make the city so much safer was very rewarding for me, and confirmed for me my interest in pursuing a career in criminal justice or homeland security. While I was unable to bring the beaten woman back to life, I found it rewarding to be able to breathe new life into her story for the eyes of the jurors to see. And I was even more gratified to know that I had helped make sure that she hadn't died in vain, that her killers were behind bars and the city was now much safer.

GREAT FIRST SENTENCES AND BEGINNINGS

The first sentence of any essay is usually the most intimidating sentence to write. But it should be the easiest. Think of it as telling one of your good friends a great (and true) story about you. Start with the most intriguing or suspenseful part of the story to get the admissions officers' attention, just as you would if you were telling your friend a real story.

SAMPLE CONVERSATION WITH FRIEND: "Did I ever tell you about the time I was in an airplane at 5,000 feet when the pilot blanked out?"

HOW THE QUESTION CAN BE TURNED AROUND TO START YOUR
ESSAY: "Just as the airplane reached an altitude of 5,000 feet,
the pilot blanked out."

SAMPLE CONVERSATION 2: Did I ever tell you about the time
when we were visiting some friends and I had just shut the front
door of their house when everything started shaking? My first
thought was that my arm was awfully powerful, but then I realized it was an earthquake.

HOW THE QUESTION CAN BE TURNED AROUND TO START YOUR
ESSAY: When I slammed the front door, everything started to
shake. Dishes tumbled out of their cabinets, and hardcover
books bounced off the·shelves. At first I marveled at my arm's
sheer power. But then I realized I was experiencing the initial
tremors of my first major earthquake.

The gist is this: Write your first sentence the way you would
start an edgy novel. Challenge the reader to worry or wonder.
Again, feel free to use first or third person.

Below are 20 interesting beginnings. Do *not* copy these sentences. Instead, use these sentences to jog your memory about
your own life experiences (and to give you plenty of "for in-
stances"). In the list below, each student's choice of a major is
included in parentheses at the end of his or her first sentence or
sentences.

1. "When I showed the village healer my impacted tooth, he
   pulled out his heaviest wooden hammer and motioned to
   me to lean back and close my eyes." *(Anthropology)*

2. "When I entered the crowded room, hundreds tried to flee
   and at least 10 were trampled to death. That's how it was on

my first day working in the chicken house." *(Animal Science, Pre-Vet)*

3. "Crack! The lightning unexpectedly struck only feet from where I was asleep in my tent in an empty field on top of a mountain. I was the tallest object for 100 yards." *(Forestry)*

4. "I confess to having been the mastermind behind the entire armed robbery. In fact I chose the weapons, selected the getaway car, and designed the whole plan. But as one who writes screenplays, I had no other way to establish my antagonist's blatant disregard for the law." *(Film Production/Screenplay Writing)*

5. "The violin's crescendo came to a crashing halt! And then suddenly a timid flute could be heard—that was the voice that I wanted the audience to identify with, when I wrote my first operatic overture." *(Music Composition)*

6. "The kind of art that I perform is magical enough to bring smiles to every member of my audience, get shy people to confess their most personal dreams, and entertain every age group non-stop for eight hours a day during the summer. I've even been known to get an applause. My art form consists of sculpting the perfect sundae at the ice-cream shop in town." *(Hospitality/Restaurant Industries)*

7. "After he kissed me onstage, my costar forgot the rest of his lines completely, and I knew I'd have to improvise for the remainder of the love scene." *(Theater Arts)*

8. "Midway through my surgery, my anesthesia wore off, but my

mouth didn't move, so I had no way to tell the doctors I was in excruciating pain." *(Public Health Management, Premed)*

9. "My Earth Science teacher dared me to swallow the snails live; he assured me it wouldn't be dangerous, and even promised me an A in the class if I complied." *(Environmental Studies)*

10. "The angry customer came into the store brandishing a knife and asking to see the manager. But that day the manager was out sick, and I had been left in charge." *(Labor Relations)*

11. "The patient who had supposedly been mute for five years suddenly began speaking. And as the hospital volunteer sent into her room to refill her pitcher, I was the only one to hear her." *(Nursing)*

12. "A life-size copy of a Rodin sculpture covered entirely with chocolate—that's what the chef brought out for dessert at the museum fund-raiser, and I was asked to make the first cut." *(Museum Administration)*

13. "The gnarled branches seemed to quiver and reach out to me in the wind, as if the tree were begging me to sketch it. So I did." *(Studio Art)*

14. "Babble for me," the interviewer demanded. "I learn a lot about people by listening to the way they speak." *(Psychology)*

15. "Though I'm too large for the seesaw and too old for the slide, one block from my house is the playground of my dreams. The Parks Department built the facility exactly to

my specifications when I won their playground design competition." *(Landscape Architecture)*

16. "I watched Dominique get eaten alive by the killer shark, and wondered what I could have done to rescue her. As a docent at the State Aquarium, it hurt to see my favorite domino fish get swallowed up with one thoughtless gulp." *(Marine Biology)*

17. "When the tornado struck my house, tossing our piano out the window, I decided to take that as a sign that I was meant for a career in meteorology—not music. I found the sheer power of the storm fascinating, something I wanted to explore further." *(Meteorology)*

18. "In my first month of business, I earned $20,000—not bad for a high school start-up." *(Business and Economics)*

19. "The night that the senator failed to show up at the rally, our master of ceremonies scanned the audience for someone who could address the thousands of people assembled. Next thing I knew, my name was called and I found myself marching up to the podium without a speech in hand." *(Public Speaking and Political Science)*

20. "The day the famous poet critiqued my work marked a significant turning point in my writing." *(English Literature)*

WRITE YOUR ESSAY NOW
Remember to Use the Five-Paragraph Format.

• **10-MINUTE BREAK** •

Grade Your Own Essay
(1 Hour)

(as if You Were an Admissions Officer) and Fix Whatever Is Wrong with It

After you have completed your essay draft, it's time to figure out your score. Here again is the scorecard. Refer to Chapter 2 if you need to be reminded of the definitions of any of the terms listed below:

HANDY SCORECARD
(for main essay)

ADD points for the following:

1. Track Record (20 points)
2. Suitable Program (15 points)
3. Contribution & Diversity (15 points)
4. Focus (10 points)
5. (You Add) Prestige (15 points)
6. Legacy (5 points)
7. Special Qualities (10 points)
8. Character (10 points)

SUBTRACT points for the following:

1. Sloppiness/Carelessness (20 points)
2. Inaccuracy (20 points)
3. Bias (20 points)

WHAT IF I FIND THAT I DON'T HAVE ENOUGH POINTS?

If you've written a wonderful essay according to the outline recommended in this book, but you feel that your score isn't high enough to get you into the college of your choice, look back on Paragraph 4 of your essay and think about what additional credentials you might add to that paragraph to increase your score. This paragraph should be filled with all of the credentials you would most want to tell the admissions officers reading your application. If done correctly, this paragraph should prove your track record (20 points). It should show each college what you have to contribute (15 points). It should demonstrate that you are focused (10 points). The last paragraph, Paragraph 5, should show the college that it has a related or suitable program to meet your needs (15 points). And as you reread your essay, you'll see that most of the essay reveals your strong character automatically (10 points). If you see any character flaws revealed, fix that (both in your essay and in your personality).

So if you write your essay correctly, at a minimum, you should be able to earn 70 points. That (in addition to great grades and standardized test scores) may be enough to get you into many of your choice colleges, if not all. If a college is only looking for students who add prestige or legacy, however, there may be nothing you can do. In that case, don't blame yourself if you're not admitted. The same is true if you don't happen to offer the "special qualities" that a particular college is seeking—you don't play bassoon or English horn; you don't fence saber, row competitively, or throw javelins; you haven't studied Ancient Greek or Sanskrit, and you don't want to major in Entomology (insects). There is no public listing of what individual colleges are seeking in different years, so there is relatively little you can do to nurture the right "special qualities" at the last minute. The best bet is to pursue those academic activities that fascinate you, and develop excellence in them over the long-term. In the meantime, earn your full 70 essay points (in addition to top grades and top standardized test scores) and you should be in good shape.

Also, have your parents or guardian proofread your essay to make sure that points aren't taken off for sloppiness, carelessness, inaccuracy, or bias. Then I'd recommend showing a draft of your essay to your high school English teacher or guidance counselor for some further polishing. (But watch out for teachers who tell you that you need to insert more of your feelings into the essay. Just by telling the story in your own words and from your own perspective, you are revealing volumes about yourself and your feelings.) You want to hand in an essay that represents you in the best light, and as accurately as possible.

The Essay-writing Process Officially Ends Here
(after 5 hours)

WHEW! CONGRATULATIONS!

Do you still have any mini essays to write or any other additional essays? If so, you might want to refer to some of the remaining chapters in this book.

Extra Chapters (For Additional Essays)

The next few chapters presume that you've already written your "main" essay for your Common Application or for any other application. These chapters focus on the three most common "extra" essays: The Diversity Essay (which many colleges request), The Most Meaningful Activity essay (which the Common Application and most colleges request), and The Why Do

You Want to Come Here? or Why Should We Accept You? essay, which most colleges request in some form or other. Writing these essays should take you much less time now that you've mastered the art of writing the kind of essays colleges prefer. In these chapters, a rubric is provided so that you get a real sense of the types of criteria admissions officers typically use to judge who gets admitted and who doesn't.

The Diversity Essay

The University of Michigan is one of many colleges and universities to specially seek out students who appreciate and who can contribute to the campus diversity. In recent years, Michigan has been known to state on its application, *"We know that diversity makes us a better university—better for learning, for teaching, and for conducting research. Share an experience through which you have gained respect for intellectual, social, or cultural differences. Comment on how your personal experiences and achievements would contribute to the diversity of the University of Michigan."*

But Michigan certainly isn't the only university seeking diversity. The Common Application has in recent years offered the opportunity to write about your diversity too, as Essay Option 5: *"A range of academic interests, personal perspectives, and life experiences adds much to the educational mix. Given your personal background, describe an experience that illustrates what you would bring to the diversity in a college community, or an encounter that demonstrated the importance of diversity to you."*

For solid students who come from populations that are underrepresented and therefore most sought after by colleges that specially seek out diversity, the diversity essay is relatively straight-forward. State in the beginning of the essay which underrepresented group you are associated with and your exact affiliation, and devote the remainder of the essay to explaining the extent of your involvement and how you could apply your knowledge of your special background to help enrich the campus. Note that most diversity-seeking colleges will want you to be specific about how you are connected to this underrepresented population in order to give you credit for diversity.

Most colleges won't be impressed with a vague response like, "I've been told that I had a great grandfather who was a Native American." (Anyone could claim that.) Instead, to have credibility, you have to explain your current tie with your Native American heritage using specifics, and the connection has to be significant (e.g., "I have lived on a Cherokee reservation throughout my high school years").

Note that some applications ask for single-paragraph diversity essays, but on the Common Application, the diversity essay is one of the full-length essay options. When you're writing a full-length diversity essay, use the format outlined in Chapter 5. (Write the full-length essay focusing on one story or experience that is somehow diversity related.)

Following is the structure for the shorter diversity mini essay.

Diversity Mini Essay Structure

SENTENCE 1: State which population you are part of that is underrepresented, and how you are affiliated with that population (through your mother's family, your father's family, your adoptive family, etc.).

SENTENCE 2-3: Explain what cultural traits or customs you have learned and/or embraced from that underrepresented tradition (languages, music, arts, religion, engineering, sciences, other knowledge and abilities).

SENTENCE 4: Explain how you can apply your special background to existing programs on campus to help enrich the campus culture (performing indigenous music at the Dreamschool Coffee House, pursuing an indigenous art form as a Dreamschool Studio Art major, sharing unique cultural perspectives as a Dreamschool Anthropology major, sharing little-known history as a Dreamschool History major, etc.).

Following are three sample essays that follow that structure:

Sample 1: As the child of two emigrants from Berushnia, I am one of the few Americans of my generation to speak fluent Berushnian and to write poetry in that melodic language. In addition, I take music lessons on the Berushnian vick harp and write lyrics in Berushnian to sing along. At Dreamschool College, I am hoping to major in Ethnomusicology to be able to publish some of the Berushnian folk tunes I have learned while growing up and perform them on campus.

Sample 2: Having spent a year in my father's native country of Gambia, I became intrigued by the colorful clothing that was manufactured there. So in addition to attending high school, I arranged to volunteer in a cotton factory to learn how the bright materials were produced, and to learn about the traditions that the different geometric patterns represented. Eventually I decided that I wanted to pursue a major in Fabric Science, having mastered the art of Gambian pattern design and wanting to share this knowledge with others who are equally passionate about fabric. At Dreamschool, I am eager to learn the different ways that materials are created throughout the world for incorporation into design of exotic clothing, upholstery, and drapery.

Sample 3: Having grandparents who still live near the coast of Ecuador, I've spent every August in their village and have become very concerned about protecting the marine wildlife there. Over the years, I have seen Ecuador become a significant tourist destination, and I'm concerned that while visitors are good for the economy, extensive diving and snorkeling may harm the coral reef. I've taken classes in conservation through Johns Hopkins summer programs, and am very involved in beach conservation efforts. At Dreamschool, I'm hoping to major in Natural Resource Policy to learn new ways to protect the environment, share some of the initiatives that we've pursued during my summers in Ecuador, and play an active role in the Marine Science Club on campus.

FOR STUDENTS WHO AREN'T CONSIDERED UNDERREPRESENTED MINORITIES

"Diversity" does not necessarily equal "underrepresented," and diversity essays aren't only meant to flag underrepresented students. Diversity can mean other characteristics as well. So if you're not a member of an underrepresented population group, don't presume that you have no diversity about which to write your essays. Colleges also seek diversity of talents, interests, skills, culture, exposure, experience, and ability to benefit from a diverse environment.

The big pitfall in the diversity essay is that applicants often reveal all kinds of hidden prejudices. I find that so many students—even the most intelligent students—don't recognize their own prejudices and biases in their writing. In trying to show their own tolerance, applicants instead inadvertently make themselves sound prejudiced. The aim of this chapter is partly to sensitize you to your own biases or biased language, so you can eliminate it.

Note that different colleges weigh and interpret diversity essays differently—just as diversity itself is valued differently by different colleges. And some colleges include the diversity question as part of the Why Should We Accept You? or Why Do You Want to Come Here? essays (described in Chapter 7), asking that you mention what you have to offer or contribute to the college by way of unique talents, abilities, or diversity.

In writing the essay, watch out for:

BIAS AND STEREOTYPING: Eliminate from your writing (and your thinking) any prejudice against any population, whether your prejudice is positive (e.g., "I've always loved poor people") or negative (e.g., "I've always hated poor people").

DEMEANING STATEMENTS: If you show in your essay that you look at other people as having inferior ways—with comparatively little or nothing to offer you intellectually in return—this demeans them. In order not to lose credibility in your essay when describing how you've helped another person or group of people, you must state what you learned or how you benefited from the two-way relationship, rather than only writing about what you invested. Bad example: "I went to Costa Rica to help build a clinic for the poor illiterate peasants there who had inadequate medical care." Good example: "I went to Costa Rica to help build a clinic, and met some fascinating villagers who shared with me some folk remedies, including a headache cure that seemed to work more effectively than our most popular headache pills."

TOKENISM: Tokenism in this case means being in contact with diverse people, but not really speaking with them or devoting any effort to understanding their thoughts, customs, or perspectives. For example, playing on a team with diverse people, but not taking the time to get to know them or have any meaningful discussions with them would constitute tokenism. Saying that you like all blue-haired people without knowing anyone with blue hair is tokenism—it's not backed up by your actions.

LACK OF DIVERSE INTERACTION: We live in a diverse society, even those of us who live in neighborhoods where everyone is of the same or similar ethnic or national ancestry and religion. Within such communities there are old people and young people, disabled and able-bodied, rich people and poor people, people with diverse political perspectives, and people with diverse talents and career choices. Some applicants are hesitant to mix with the variety of people available to them—they avoid involvement with people who aren't like-minded. Others seek out people with diverse perspectives and thus learn more about themselves and the world that way. Public universities and religiously (and culturally) unaffiliated colleges are generally more attracted to students who deliberately pursue involvement with diverse people. These students are seen as most likely to benefit most from the larger university environment.

TASTELESS COMPARISON: In this case it means comparing the way an individual or population looks or behaves to some stereotypical caricature (e.g., Aunt Jemima, Uncle Ben, Sambo, etc.).

ALL AMERICAN CITIZENS ARE AMERICANS: They are all equally American and American-looking. For those who claim otherwise, we take off points.

CONFUSING OR MIXING UP CULTURES: Confusing Chinese, Japanese, and Korean cultures results in a deduction of points.

> NOTE: A badly written diversity essay can exclude you from admission, even if your grades, standardized test scores, and main essay are A-plus work.

BAD ESSAYS

I'm very comfortable with people who are mainstream Americans as well as people who aren't mainstream and I'm extremely tolerant of different cultures. One of the guys on my soccer team is Oriental. His grandfather came here from Asia, and we get along fine. I even like Chinese food a lot, and we order in Chinese after some of our practices. Once, he even showed us how to use chopsticks. We have some other non-Americans living in our neighborhood as well. There's an Arab American family, but they keep to themselves a lot, but I'm careful to invite the Arab boy out to practice with us just the same. In college, I would invite kids who aren't mainstream to join in activities too.

WHAT MAKES THIS ESSAY BAD? It violates the rule that "All Americans are Americans." It refers to the Arab American family as "non-Americans." It implies that the Arab boy isn't "mainstream American." It assumes that the "Oriental" teammate is Chinese, when he might easily be of a different Asian background. And the writer shows his appreciation of Asian culture to be very tokenistic—limited to Chinese food and chopsticks—and his relationship with people of cultures other than his own to be tokenistic.

When I traveled to Belize to help villagers build a day-care center, I was surprised at how primitive the conditions were. The so-called showers had very primitive plumbing, and the floors of the houses were untiled— just solid cement. The people only ate rice and beans most of the time. But despite the primitive conditions, the people seemed very friendly and appreciative that sophisticated Americans would take the time to come to their underdeveloped village to build a day-care center. It just shows that you don't have to be cosmopolitan to be nice. Being among these simple people, who spoke no English, taught me the value of diversity. I would bring that knowledge with me to college.

WHAT MAKES THE ABOVE ESSAY BAD? Although the writer has some kind words to say in the end, the essay is very condescending and demeaning of the villagers. The relationship of the author to the people in the village is superficial and tokenistic. The author doesn't write about a single interaction he/she has enjoyed during the visit, and has no real appreciation of the culture or the personalities.

Last summer I worked at McDonald's with an African American jazz enthusiast, a Korean American who preferred to bring his own Chinese food with him to work, and an Indian girl whose mother was a vegetarian. We also had a Hispanic boy, and we were all impressed with how quickly Hispanics work. But despite our differences, we managed to get along okay behind the counter. In fact, having different people around me made me feel more comfortable when other minorities would come into the McDonald's to order hamburgers, and so I learned to appreciate having diverse people around me and hope to have a similar setting in college.

WHAT MAKES THE ABOVE ESSAY BAD? This essay is filled with reinforcements of stereotypes, generalizations (about the speed that Hispanics work) and bias. And once again, the writer is likely confusing Korean culture with Chinese culture. The reader doesn't get the impression that the applicant really gained any appreciation for any of the cultures of the fellow workers.

As a member of my church mission group, I've traveled to many diverse communities preaching and praying for diverse people. This has exposed me to many diverse cultures that I wouldn't normally get to see. I find it very rewarding to be able to help them, and I know they are very grateful for my prayers.

WHAT MAKES THE ABOVE ESSAY BAD? The reader gets the impression that the applicant views all diverse populations condescendingly, as people to pray for or to preach to. Although the applicant clearly travels a lot, we don't get the impression that the applicant has gained any appreciation for the diverse cultures to which he/she has been exposed.

Although my community is entirely Caucasian, our church has invited other churches to share an annual interfaith service with us—and sometimes we have shared services with other ethnic groups. One year we were invited to a joint service at a black Baptist church. It was so interesting to see how much more lively the black service was with lots of singing and even dancing. In fact, I enjoyed that service immensely and would like to go back there sometime. I'm hoping my church will plan another joint service there someday.

WHAT MAKES THE ABOVE ESSAY BAD? Although it sounds at first like the applicant is making a positive statement, the writer seems to remain an outsider. She clearly keeps her distance, not really giving any evidence that she's mingling with the people in the black church—in fact, she tells us that she is waiting for her church to plan another interfaith service, rather than make her own arrangements to visit the black Baptist church on her own. Ultimately she comes across as biased, rather than genuine.

Even though I'd describe myself as a typical American, I like hanging out with Jewish kids and Asian kids a lot because they are all smart—especially at math and science. There are many of these minorities in my school, and I try to study as hard as they do, because these populations tend to be very successful in engineering and business—two fields that I am considering for my career.

WHAT MAKES THE ABOVE ESSAY BAD? Although the stereotyping at first sounds flattering—calling "Jewish kids and Asian kids . . . smart," all ethnic stereotyping (including "positive prejudice") is considered bad and biased. Also, the reader describes himself as "a typical American," implying that these other students cannot be considered typical Americans. Applicants should avoid referring to themselves or anyone else as "typical," in that one of the points of these essays is to see how well the applicant appreciates that America is a very diverse country that values diversity, and that no one ethnic group or religion constitutes "a typical American." Instead, typical Americans come in all shapes, sizes, hair colors, eye colors, and skin colors, and with the widest varieties of ethnic and national roots.

I don't care what background people are from, as long as they believe in one God. After all, America is "one nation under God," so we're all God's children—brown, black, yellow, pink, or white.

WHAT MAKES THE ABOVE ESSAY BAD? While at first glimpse, it might seem that the applicant is very tolerant of all different races and religions, the applicant clearly states that he is only tolerant of those who believe in one God. That excludes a lot of his classmates. At most universities, there are many students who are nonbelievers, many who would describe themselves as agnostic, and many students who believe in multiple gods as part of their family religion.

WEAK ESSAYS (NOT VERY IMPRESSIVE)

My lacrosse team at school consists of white students, black students, and Hispanic students, all working together to win. While we come from different neighborhoods and social crowds and have different friends off the field, when we're on the field, we have all learned to put cultural differences aside to work for a common goal. Although I'm one of the white students, we all respect one another as athletes. And through this cooperation, we've maintained our winning streak.

WHAT MAKES THIS ESSAY WEAK? While the applicant doesn't show blatant racism or bias, the writer also doesn't show the reader any real appreciation for other cultures. In fact, he makes a point of dissociating himself, saying that he lives in a "different" neighborhood and mingles with "different . . . social crowds." He only advocates cooperation as a tactic to win. As a result, his essay comes across as tokenistic and self-serving.

––––––––

Every Saturday morning I play violin in a youth orchestra that attracts a large diversity of students from all over the county. Some come from inner-city neighborhoods, others come from rural farmlands. Together, we play Beethoven and Mozart as well as contemporary ethnic music written by composers from China, Kenya, and Brazil. The string section alone has students who trace their ancestry to 15 different nationalities. But all of these diverse students are able to work together to create beautiful harmony.

WHAT MAKES THIS ESSAY WEAK? Although the applicant writes a nonoffensive essay and is able to cite multiple nationalities and varied settings where students live, the reader doesn't get the impression that the applicant has any real appreciation for who these other players are, or even an appreciation for the diversity of the music they play together. To this applicant, the diversity is just a matter of convenience and tokenism. We don't hear of any close friendships or bonds with the other players, and we don't sense any attachment to the exotic music of China, Kenya, or Brazil. He seems to only like intercultural cooperation as a means of finding people to play the other instruments.

I have learned to appreciate diversity through the foods I eat from all over the world. My parents both work, so on weekdays we like to keep our meals simple. Monday is spaghetti night—that comes from Italy. Tuesday is Chinese food night, and we order in. Wednesday we usually order in Sicilian pizza. Thursday is for tacos—we go to Taco Bell. And on Friday, we usually eat American food—boring meatloaf or hamburgers—so we don't forget our roots. I especially like Jewish rye, Greek olives, French cheese, Polish kielbasa, and German sauerkraut.

WHAT MAKES THIS ESSAY WEAK? Again, the essay is not offensive toward any group, but mentioning food does not indicate any real appreciation of diversity. In fact, the foods themselves are basically American fast foods, and the references to them are tokenistic and don't entail any appreciation of diverse cultures or cuisines.

Okay Essays

My family is Estonian American but we speak English at home. Living in a community that consists largely of emigrants from Finland, Sweden, and Denmark, I am a minority in my school, but not many kids know it. I have managed to fit in with all of the school's social organizations and within our community. Although I attend an Estonian church, all of my other activities include a diversity of ethnic groups, and I'm very comfortable with that.

WHAT MAKES THIS ESSAY JUST OKAY? We don't get a sense that the writer has a real appreciation for diversity—his emphasis seems to be wanting to fit in. And all of the cultures he cites are Scandinavian, not a major venture geographically away from Estonia. But he shows that he has some ethnic identity, as an

Estonian churchgoer. Perhaps he'll share some of his culture with the campus.

———————

Having grown up in a big city, I am accustomed to having classes with ethnically diverse students, and living in an apartment building with a wide diversity of tenants. Our building has decorations for every holiday tradition. And in the evening, around dinnertime, you can smell just about every kind of food from the hallway—everyone preparing his or her own ethnic meals. In the elevator, you can hear lots of different languages spoken. For me, diversity is just an assumed way of life.

WHAT MAKES THIS ESSAY JUST OKAY? The applicant doesn't take any action to pursue or embrace diversity. We don't learn anything about the applicant's own contributions to or appreciation of diversity. We get the impression that she is just passive and has little to contribute.

THE BEST ESSAYS

I spend two hours every day after school volunteering at the local senior home, visiting with old people who otherwise go unvisited. Some have younger family members who live far away in other parts of the country or other parts of the world. I find these visits to be very enlightening, as I hear about their experiences during some of the events that I've read about in history books: Margaret tells me about the Great Depression; Oscar tells me about growing up in Ukraine during World War II. Albert told me about life before television and air-conditioning. Intergenerational friendships are among the diverse friendships I have especially learned to value and enjoy.

This applicant chooses to focus on intergenerational diversity. And although that's an easier subject than addressing racial, ethnic, sexual, or religious diversity, she would not lose points for this essay. She comes across as a caring person who will get along well with diverse students and professors alike on campus.

———

In my high school, I'm the president of the GLBT organization, where students of different sexual orientations come together to discuss our diversity and school policies. Sometimes the club just provides a refuge from the straight world and a place to talk freely for students who don't fit in. We devote most of our meetings to planning assemblies and programs for the entire school to help sensitize them to our situation, and to show them that we have much to contribute to the school community. I envision myself continuing this involvement through the Dreamschool GLBT Club in college.

This applicant chooses to focus on sexual diversity—a difficult subject in most parts of the United States. The applicant makes it clear how she intends to contribute to campus diversity through continued involvement in GLBT activities and program planning.

———

My younger sister is deaf, and as a result, my whole family has made a point of learning American Sign Language and becoming involved in the deaf community. I tutor elementary-school-age deaf students once a week in math and reading. In addition, I have formed close bonds with some of my peers at the Central School for the Deaf, including my best friend, Eva. I love the fact that knowing ASL has let me into a whole diverse world—with a culture of its own—that most hearing people know little about.

This applicant focuses on diversity of physical ability and deaf culture. This kind of essay works very well, and shows a genuine involvement with a diverse culture.

Being the only Asian American in a Caucasian community was very difficult for me as a child. Other kids would make fun of the way I looked because they didn't know any other Asians. But when I entered high school and tried out for the wrestling team (and made it), I earned the respect of everyone at school. I became the hero, made lots of friends, and was no longer viewed as an oddity. I prefer a college setting with total diversity, where nobody stands out as the only minority. I enjoy sharing my own Thai cultural background and learning about other people's cultures—especially the cultural celebrations. But even if I'm a minority of one, I've learned how to adjust and even thrive.

As long as the story has a happy ending, this kind of essay about successfully facing discrimination works. Students who never adjust to their setting (unless they're in some dangerous or impossibly discriminatory environment) are less appealing to colleges. An important element of this essay is the reference to sharing one's culture with others.

Every Monday night I take 3-D art lessons at the local community center. My class consists of women of all different ages and backgrounds. We usually talk while we create, and we share our various artistic backgrounds. Some have kids or even grandkids my age, and I find this cultural and intergenerational mixing to be more exciting than the lesson itself. Akiko, who sits next to me, comes from Japan, and has taken classes in Japanese brush painting. Gioia comes from a family of glassmakers in Venice, Italy, and helped with my glass fusion sculpture. Emma studied stone carving in Finland and showed me some helpful techniques of sculpting alabaster, and Anastasia taught us Easter egg decorating from her native Ukraine. I'm the only American-born student in the class—and I now have so many artistic traditions to bring with me to college.

This essay works nicely, demonstrating that the applicant is really interacting with diverse people, learning new traditions, and appreciating some of the highlights of diverse cultures.

I was born in Latvia, and my family moved to the States when I was 12. As a result, I spent most of my middle and high school years telling people where Latvia was, sharing some of my family's traditions, and making friends in an urban science magnet school that is largely Chinese, Korean, and Jewish. Through hard work, I have gained the respect of my peers, and also the friendship. In fact, I've taken Chinese as my high school language, and am currently taking AP Chinese, elementary Korean, and earning the top grades in the class.

This essay tells the reader of the applicant's diverse background and also about her successful integration into and appreciation of the diverse culture at high school.

In my International Folk Dance class, we are learning dances from all over the world. I love the diversity of dance, and celebrate each new exotic step that I learn—and each new culture that contributes. I especially enjoy some of the Baltic line dances and the energy of the Israeli circle dances that don't require a partner. I like the grace of the Greek dances, particularly Misirlou. I also have taught the group two of my favorite Hungarian dances. At the end of each year, we perform before spectators in the public park. For that show, we're each expected to wear the traditional clothing of our different heritages. Together, we make a very colorful group. I wear my Hungarian costume proudly.

The applicant speaks of her own contribution to the diversity of folk dance and affirms her appreciation of the contribution of other cultures.

———————

I'm a mixture of everything, and I am the product of total diversity. My father's parents are Native American and Native Hawaiian Islander. My mother's parents are black Hispanic from the Dominican Republic and Irish. I'm the official melting pot. As one who was brought up to celebrate a wide variety of traditions, I would especially enjoy a campus that values diversity. A trained folk musician, I play the ukulele as well as the Irish flute, and I would love to participate in the Dreamschool Folk Music Ensemble.

While this last essay is clearly written by someone who is associated with several underrepresented populations, he lets the reader know that he has mastered some ethnic artistic traditions (his folk music) to contribute. This makes the essay much stronger.

In reviewing all of the diversity essays, note that there are lots of different forms of diversity. Also note that the essays that mention what the candidate has accomplished or the skills that the candidate has acquired, tend to be much stronger than the others. While many applicants choose to write about ethnic diversity and their own ethnic folk traditions, you should not feel limited to that theme.

The Why Do You Want to Come Here? Essay

Many applications ask you to explain your choice of college in a mini essay—sometimes 150 words or fewer. As a result, many applicants blow this off as an unimportant essay—**BIG MISTAKE.** Many of the most competitive colleges view this mini essay to be the most important essay—the deciding factor.

Why is this essay so important to competitive colleges? The gist is this: They get so many applications that fall within their "range" (meaning the right GPA and the right standardized test scores). So how do they figure out which students to take? They prefer the students who most want *them* for what *they* offer. So they read the Why Do You Want to Come Here? essays, combing through to find those students who are really serious about an interest in the specific college and have taken the time to fully explore the opportunities that the college offers. Admissions officers figure that if you've taken the time to explore what their college has to offer now, before you're admitted, you'll likely hit the ground running (taking advantage of all the opportunities) once you are admitted.

So let's start by looking at how the overwhelming majority of students respond to this essay question (unless they read this book or someone savvy edits their work).

HERE'S THE TYPICAL (BAD) RESPONSE:

Ever since I was in kindergarten, I knew I wanted to attend Dreamschool College. The professors are very smart—some have even won Nobel Prizes. And the college has an outstanding reputation and lots of prestige, all of which is very deserved. I fit in perfectly with the students, who are also very smart and have a lot of school spirit. I also like the attractive campus—especially the new fitness center—and even the weather matches what I want perfectly. I can easily envision myself living in the freshman dormitory, playing video games with the other students, and studying each night in the awesome library, which has more books than anyone can possibly read. On weekends, I would volunteer to tutor local children, and I would sing with the college chorus. When I visited the campus, I felt the magic immediately. Everything just felt right. And this confirmed for me that Dreamschool College was indeed my dream college. Go Dreamers!

WHAT'S WRONG WITH THAT ESSAY? The big problem is that it's completely generic. That means that it could be sent to practically any college that has a campus (any campus) and a reasonably new fitness center. (If the campus doesn't have a fitness center, the student could just substitute the words "science center" or "student center," or whatever the newest building is on campus, without a whole lot of research and effort.)

In other words, this essay shows the college that the student didn't take any time at all to really research what the college has to offer. So this okay-sounding essay spells "Instant Reject," because the applicant demonstrates that he or she is too lazy to even look up what the college is about. The applicant clearly is just plugging in this essay for every application. Such an essay shows no real passion for what Dreamschool has to offer—the student doesn't even *know* what Dreamschool has to offer.

Here is another bad example:

Ever since I set eyes on Dreamschool, I knew it was right for me. When I arrived on campus, the sun was shining, the bells in the campus chapel were playing the song "Welcome Stranger, You're No Stranger to Me," and I can't describe how welcome I felt. I just looked at my mother and she winked back. She knew exactly what I was thinking. That's one of my favorite songs, so we both felt like that was a sign that I belonged at Dreamschool. During my visit, I met all these really nice kids in the dorm where I stayed who were just like me. They wore the same Abercrombie clothes like I do. They stayed up till midnight studying like I do. And even the cafeteria food in the main dorm had a salad bar with artichokes. I love artichokes. I bought myself a Dreamschool T-shirt in the book store—I love the Dreamschool colors and have since worn the shirt proudly back at high school. But the highlight was when I sat in on a class and understood what the professor was saying. Suddenly I could envision myself as a real student at Dreamschool. I fit in perfectly. Nobody in the room even knew that I'm still in high school.

The one positive element that this essay offers is that the student apparently went to visit the Dreamschool campus. Some colleges—particularly small liberal arts colleges—prefer to accept students who make a point of visiting their campus. But after the visit, this applicant focuses on all the wrong reasons for wanting to attend Dreamschool, so the essay is extremely weak. Nowhere does the applicant mention her academic interests or how she would use the academic resources provided by the campus. She bases her entire essay on music that happened to be playing, clothing, and food.

HERE ARE SOME QUICK RULES ABOUT THE
WHY DO YOU WANT TO COME HERE? ESSAY

RULE 1: This essay should be tailored to each college you're applying to. (Change the essay each time you apply to a different college. Yes, that will take up a lot of time. But this is supposed to be
the most time-consuming part of the application. Unlike the main
essay, which you could just plug in to practically every application,
this essay requires individual tailoring.) If you send a generic response (the same response) to each college, then each college will
know you don't care, and you'll get a slew of rejections.

RULE 2: This essay should focus mainly on academics—majors,
courses, professors, research opportunities, internships, and
student activities that tie in with your academic interests. How
do you find out what majors, courses, and opportunities they
offer? Go to each college website, one at a time, and go to Academics. From there, find a list of Majors or Departments, and
choose two majors that interest you the most. Then go to those
majors' websites to see what those Majors/Departments offer in
the way of courses and opportunities.

Within each Major/Department website, look at the tab that
lists Courses. Also look at every tab that shows Special Programs,
Research, Travel Abroad, Field Experiences, or Interdepartmental Opportunities. In other words, you want to find out
every single opportunity that your selected majors offer. Choose
the opportunities that appeal to you most and that coincide
with your experience so far (track record). Those are the opportunities to mention in your mini essay. Those are the right
reasons that you want to attend that college.

Emory University is kind enough to give its applicants some
hints about what not to include in the essay. On Emory's supplemental application, the following essay prompt has been used

in recent years: "*Many students decide to apply to Emory University based on our size, location, reputation, and yes, the weather. Besides these valid reasons as a possible college choice, why is Emory University a particularly good match for you?*" Follow the restrictions that Emory suggests for *all* of your applications to *all* colleges.

RULE 3: If you mention student activities, mention them by name. Do not say, "I want to audition for the college orchestra and band." Instead say, "I want to audition for the Dreamschool Symphony Orchestra and the Dreamers Marching Band." That demonstrates that you showed enough interest to take the time to look up the names of the college ensembles.

RULE 4: Use the language of the college (which you learn by checking out the college website). When you mention the name of a major, course, or activity, get the name right!

- Don't call it a "major," if the college calls it a "concentration." (Don't say, "I want to major in Chemistry," if people at the college say, "I want to concentrate in Chemistry.") At Harvard, for example, people "concentrate"; they don't "major."
- Don't use the word "course" to mean "subject" or "class," if the college only uses the word "course" to refer to the name of a "major" (as in "What course are you majoring in?"). At MIT, for example, people major in a "course," not a "subject."
- Don't call your intended major Neuroscience, if the name of the department is Brain Science or Cognitive Science. Don't call it Biology, if they refer to it as Life Sciences or Biological Sciences.
- Don't say you want to join the Dreamschool Symphony Orchestra if the name of the group is the Dreamschool College Orchestra.

RULE 5: All of your answers should mesh with your track record so far. You shouldn't say that you want to apply as a Business major if you've never before taken a business class or experienced business. Don't say you want to join the Debate Team if you've never debated in high school. Such desires lack credibility. (Colleges would ask, "If you're so interested in business or debate, why isn't there any business or debate listed on your application under Activities, Courses, or even Summers?")

RULE 6: Note that many colleges also ask—as part of the same question—what you can contribute to their college. The question may be phrased like, "What makes you a perfect match for our college?" You need to know that a perfect match is two-sided. They can help you, but you need to also have something to offer them. So when the essay asks about a "perfect match," you need to cite somewhere in the essay how you can contribute your talents and skills to help the college.

Here is a list of answers to avoid writing. When you write your own essay, take off 10 points for each of these answers, if they show up in your essay.

BAD ANSWERS (WHAT MOST STUDENTS WRITE)

1. SMART PROFESSORS (deduct 10 points):
   • You have high-powered Nobel Prize winners on your faculty.
   • I've heard that professors invite the students home to dinner.

2. SMART STUDENTS (deduct 10 points):
   • When I'm around smart students, I work hard; when I'm not, I languish.
   • I'm heavily influenced by the crowd of kids I get in with.
   • I enjoy my classes more when I'm surrounded by smart students.

3. THE NAME, THE CAR DECAL, AND THE T-SHIRT
   (deduct 10 points):
   - I can't wait to drive my car around with the decal and wear the T-shirt.
   - Dreamschool College has a great name—like Yale.

4. REPUTATION (deduct 10 points):
   - Dreamschool College has the best reputation.
   - You're ranked among the top 20 in *U.S. News & World Report.*
   - I want to apply to medical school, and Dreamschool is good for my résumé.

5. SCHOOL SPIRIT (deduct 10 points):
   - I prefer a school with lots of team spirit—Go Dreamers!
   - I want a rah-rah school, and I've always been a fan of the Dreamers.
   - For my 12th birthday, my parents bought me a shirt with the school colors.

6. GENERIC ACTIVITIES (deduct 10 points):
   - I want Dreamschool College so I may join a community service club.
   - I am eager to try out for the chorus and participate in the active social life.
   - I plan to join a fraternity and do a year abroad.

7. CLIMATE (deduct 10 points):
   - I love crisp fall days and dark snowy winters to get me in the mood to study.
   - I can only work on sunny 90-degree days, so the climate is perfect.

8. LOCATION AND SIZE (deduct 10 points):
   - I prefer a small campus in the country with no distractions.
   - I prefer a large campus in the city with lots of nearby entertainment options.

9. FRIENDS/COUSINS ON CAMPUS (deduct 10 points):
   - I'm just like my friend Tiffany, and she's happy there, so I would be too.
   - My cousin goes there and we're hoping to room or commute together.
   - All the kids from my camp/school/club/neighborhood go there to college.
   - Four of my cousins got into Dreamschool, and I'm every bit as smart.

10. FRIENDS/COUSINS NEAR THE CAMPUS (deduct 10 points):
    - My parents' best friends live a mile from the campus in case of any problems.
    - My girlfriend goes to college just down the road, so this would be perfect.

11. ARCHITECTURE (deduct 10 points):
    - The ivy-covered architecture on campus reminds me of Harvard.
    - I can really envision myself studying in the campus library every day.
    - I love how the buildings all match; the buildings are all my style.

12. FITTING IN (deduct 10 points):
    - I wear Abercrombie, and all the students on campus wear Abercrombie too.

- I sat in on a class, and a professor mistook me for another student, so I fit in.
- All the kids play computer games and so do I, so I'd fit in perfectly.
- I've already picked out my fraternity.

13. **ALWAYS WANTED TO GO THERE** (deduct 10 points):
    - Ever since I was 5, I knew I wanted to go to Dreamschool College.
    - Since I attended soccer camp on campus, I knew this was the college for me.
    - I've always been a Dreamschool girl.

14. **COMMON MAJORS** (deduct 10 points):
    - I want to major in Biology, and your college offers Biology.
    - I want to major in Economics, and your college offers Economics.

15. **COMMON GENERIC PROGRAMS** (deduct 10 points):
    - I want Dreamschool, because you offer study abroad, and I love to travel.
    - I want Dreamschool so I can benefit from your Writing Lab.
    - I hear you have interesting research.

16. **GENERAL FLATTERY** (deduct 10 points):
    - I've always known that Dreamschool was the greatest.
    - Dreamschool is only for the "cream of the crop," the elite of the elite.

17. SLOPPINESS (deduct 10 points):
    - I am applying as a perspective Premed major at
      Dreamcollege.
    - I'm interested in studying Artic whales and other fish.

18. INACCURACY (deduct 10 points)
    - I'm especially attracted to the semester abroad in
      New Mexico.
    - As a debate team captain, I'd be eager to major in
      Forensic Science.
    - I always wanted to study Government in the State of
      Washington DC.

19. BIAS (deduct 10 points)
    - I like the fact that the campus is mostly preppies with no
      blue hair or tattoos.
    - I prefer colleges with higher percentages of real
      Americans and fewer ethnics.
    - I picked Dreamschool for its liberal political reputation.

20. TEACHING THE COLLEGE Don't tell a college what it offers.
     (deduct 10 points):
    - Dreamschool has a Gehry building on campus,
      enhancing its architecture.
    - Dreamschool has one of the most innovative programs in
      entomology.

To fix those Teaching the College two sentences so you don't
lose 10 points, insert at the beginning of each sentence "What I
like about Dreamschool is that . . ." Then the sentence is no
longer merely telling the college what it offers. Instead it's
telling the college what you like about what it offers, and that
makes a big difference.

Good: As a prospective Architecture major, what I like about Dreamschool is that it has a Gehry building on campus, enhancing its architecture.

Good: What I like about Dreamschool is that it has one of the most innovative programs in entomology.

GOOD (ACADEMIC) ANSWERS TO WHY YOU WANT TO GO TO DREAMSCHOOL COLLEGE

Notice that there aren't as many good answers as there are bad answers. I advise students to stick with academic answers—your essays should discuss why the courses and academic programs match your credentials. Exceptions: When students are recruitable for a sport or musical instrument, it's okay to discuss athletic facilities/programs and musical ensembles, but also mention academics. Use this essay to try to show how the college's offerings coincide with who you are and your track record from high school.

1. TRACK RECORD (15 points): On most applications, very little space is allotted for the Why Do You Want to Come Here? essay, so you can't hope to summarize all of your résumé or credentials within this mini essay. At the same time, you should try to squeeze in at least one relevant credential along with each reason that you want to go to Dreamschool College—to show the admissions officers that Dreamschool matches your credentials perfectly. To illustrate this, see the bold face Track Record descriptions below. (e.g., If you say you want to go to Dreamschool College to major in Public Policy and you have some policy experience or background, give yourself 15 points for track record. If you say that you want to study Modeling, but you show no evidence of ever having modeled before, then give yourself zero for track record.)

2. UNIQUE/RIGHT MAJORS (that coincide with your track record) (15 points):

- **Having volunteered at a local hospital,** I want to major in a combination of Neuroscience and Immunology, and Dreamschool is one of the few colleges to offer this combination to undergraduates.
- I want to major in Peace Studies from a Quaker perspective, and Dreamschool is one of the few colleges to offer that approach.
- **Having tinkered with car engines throughout high school,** I want to combine studies in Engineering and Entrepreneurship, and Dreamschool offers those subjects as a double major.

3. UNIQUE/RIGHT COURSES (that coincide with your track record) (10 points):

- **Having worked in a café for three summers,** I am eager to take The Wines of France, which only Dreamschool offers.
- **As a volunteer docent at the planetarium,** I'm eager to take the course on Dark Matter, a topic that totally fascinates me.
- **Having studied Shakespeare's comedies in high school,** I am now eager to take Dreamschool's Shakespeare's Tragedies course and also Jane Austen.

4. UNIQUE/SUITABLE PROGRAMS (that coincide with your track record) (10 points):

- As a prospective Urban Studies major, I like the fact that Dreamschool offers semester-long internships in City Planning in Chicago.
- **Having organized two fund-raisers,** I would be thrilled to

attend the Fund-Raiser Seminar in Spain as part of Dreamschool's major in Nonprofits.

- **Having worked at the clothing store for two years,** I'm very excited about the retail summer internships Dreamschool offers in New York.

5. COMPELLING NEED: (family medical need; only school with your major) (10 points)

- **As one who takes care of his grandfather every day after school** just two blocks from the campus, my family needs me to attend Dreamschool.
- **As a Lyme disease patient at Dreamschool Clinic,** I am very much hoping to attend Dreamschool College to continue my treatment while studying.
- **As the National Checkers Champion,** I want to go to Dreamschool to help you run the National Checkers Tournament.

6. PROFESSORS (whose work you know) (5 points)

- **Having read all of Prof. John Smith's books on Thomas Jefferson,** I would savor the opportunity to take his Jeffersonian Era course and hear the professor's lectures on Jefferson's decisions.
- **Having performed in two of Prof. Jane Smith's plays,** I would love to take her play-writing course and get her feedback on my scripts.

7. LEGACY (parents or grandparents) (10 points):

- My grandfather always spoke fondly about his years at Dreamschool College.

- My mother always let me help her plan her Dreamschool reunions.

8. RESEARCH PROGRAMS (relevant to your major) (10 points):

- **Having tutored history for two years,** I would love to conduct original research in art history through Dreamschool's museum internships.
- **Having conducted materials science research and entered the Siemens Competition with a research paper,** I'm eager to explore nanotechnology research at Dreamschool.

9. SUITABLE ACTIVITIES (ACADEMIC CLUBS AND ORGANIZATIONS) (10 points):

- **As one who was active in mural painting in high school,** I am eager to join Dreamschool's Mural Club, one of the few such clubs in America.
- **Having mastered the "koto,"** I especially would want to audition for the Ancient Chinese Music Ensemble, one of a few such groups in the world.
- **As captain of my high school varsity water polo team,** I would try out for Dreamschool's varsity team—one of the few East Coast women's varsity water polo teams.

10. MEANINGFUL/QUALITY CAMPUS VISIT (Sitting in on classes, meeting with professors, talking with students—not just looking at the campus sights) (5 points):

- **Having visited the campus,** attended an Art History class, and met with Prof. Joan Higgins, I know Dreamschool is where I want to study Egyptian art.
- **Having worked with Prof. Jones last summer, I got to**

attend campus botany lectures, and know this would be the best place for me to explore botany.

11. YOUR CONTRIBUTION (if the application question asks why you'd be a "perfect fit" or "perfect match" for the college) (10 additional points):

- **As captain of my high school Math Team,** I could help Dreamschool continue its remarkable record in the Putnam Competition.
- **As an accomplished French horn player,** I would be eager to perform with the Dreamschool Pit Orchestra.

Applications need to be consistent, so if you've already selected a major at this college for another one of your essays or if the college asked you what you wanted to major in and you listed your choice, stick with that answer for this essay too.

If this is the first essay you're writing for your application, then choose an appropriate major from the college's website. Choose a major that matches your track record, instead of one that matches your dreams. So, for example, if you are a student who led the Classics Club in high school and want to major in Biology, your odds might be significantly better if you apply as a Classics major, rather than a Biology major, since that's where you have a proven track record, and that would seem to be where your true interests lie.

To do the best job on this essay, go to the college's website and make a list of what appeals to you about the college academically—especially qualities that the college possesses that no other colleges possess. If you already told the college what you want to major in earlier in the application (and wrote your general Common Application essay to reflect that major), stick with that major—so you don't contradict yourself!

HANDY SCORECARD

(only for the **Why Do You Want to Come Here?** essay)

ADD points for the following:

1. Track Record   (15 points)
2. Right Major   (15 points)
3. Right Courses   (10 points)
4. Suitable Programs   (10 points)
5. Compelling Need   (10 points)
6. Profs Whose Work You Know (5 points)
7. Legacy   (10 points)
8. Research/Field   (10 points)
   Opportunities
9. Suitable Activities   (10 points)
10. Quality Campus Visit Cited (5 points)
11. Your Contribution   (10 points)

SUBTRACT 10 points for examples of each of the following:

1. Smart Professors
2. Smart Students
3. Name, Decal, T-shirt
4. Reputation
5. School Spirit
6. Generic Activities
7. Climate
8. Location and Size
9. Friends/Cousins on Campus
10. Friends/Cousins Near Campus
11. Architecture
12. Fitting In
13. Always Wanted to Go There
14. Common Majors
15. Common (Generic) Programs
16. General Flattery
17. Sloppiness/Carelessness
18. Inaccuracy
19. Bias
20. Teaching the College

SAMPLE GOOD ESSAYS

To get you started, here are some sample good essays that meet the challenge well. You can use the same overall format. But do your own research to find specific courses and programs that match your unique interests.

Sample Good Essay 1: Dreamschool College is my first choice for college because it's the only top school to offer a major in Ornithology plus a solid core curriculum. Having participated in an expedition to study the language of tropical birds with Earthwatch, and having taken a college credit course in ornithology at Central University, I have built the most solid credentials available to benefit from Dreamschool's program. I would likely minor in Botany, and take the course called Flowers that Attract Birds. I would also be thrilled to participate in Dreamschool's Field Studies Program on the Orkney Islands, the Undergraduate Research Involvement Program, and the Undergraduate Mathematics Society. I envision myself actively involved in the college Birding Club—one of the few competitive college birding organizations—as well as the Dreamschool Greenhouse Club.

Sample Good Essay 2: As an avid computer enthusiast who designed my own computer game during high school, my dream is to major in Computer Science at Dreamschool College School of Engineering. Having already read the texts by Prof. John Smith and Prof. Robert Jones, I know I would thrill at the opportunity to take programming classes with these two famous computer scientists. I know I would become very involved in Dreamschool's Undergraduate Research Involvement Program, in which I would want to conduct original research on building nanocomputers. In addition, I would join Dreamschool's chapter of IEEE Computer Club, and I would volunteer as a computer tutor in the Dreamschool Computer Lab. I also know I'd be very involved in the Anime Society and the Computer Gaming Club.

Sample Good Essay 3: What excites me most about Dreamschool College is its major in Entrepreneurship. Having led fund-raisers and started my own small clothing-related businesses throughout high school—I design my own clothes—I find entrepreneurship fascinating. I am especially eager to take courses like Fashion Start-ups, Organizing Fashion Events, Business Accounting, and Import-Export Regulations. In addition, I like the fact that Dreamschool would let me take a full liberal arts curriculum. In the Art Department, I would take classes in fashion design. In Economics, I would take the course on The Clothing Industry. And in the Materials Science Department, I would take a course on Fabric Science. In addition, I would be very active in Dreamschool's Fashion Club and pursue an internship through the Undergrad Internship Program at a clothing design firm in New York City.

Sample Good Essay 4: As one who has always loved French culture and who scored 750 on my French SAT II, I am drawn to Dreamschool College for its outstanding French Literature Program—I definitely want to major in French. I especially like the department's voluntary Drill Program, which drills students in French conversation and conjugations every morning at 9. I'm sure I would show up loyally to keep improving my fluency. I also love the fact that Dreamschool maintains a Maison Française, where students may attend luncheons weekly to practice their French and sample some real French cooking. And I would be thrilled to spend my junior year in France through the Junior Year Abroad Program, studying language and literature in Paris and Grenoble. I can't imagine a more exciting undergraduate experience. I envision myself active in the French Club, and also want to take Art History courses, Linguistics, and possibly some Latin.

Sample Good Essay 5: The fact that Dreamschool College is one of the few universities to offer Architecture as a major to undergraduates is what I find most appealing about Dreamschool. As one who grew up in a populated city, I am fascinated with architecture. For the last three summers,

I've attended architecture summer programs at colleges, including last summer, when I finally got to attend Dreamschool's prestigious Architecture Program for High School Students. Working with Prof. John Smith, I designed and built a model of a museum, a theater, and a public library—all part of my application portfolio. What I like most about the Dreamschool approach is that the required courses emphasize construction engineering as well as design. Outside the department, I'm eager to take Urban Planning and Civil Engineering courses as well. I would thrill at the chance to do an architecture internship as part of the Junior Internship Program, and to participate in the study tour of Ancient Roman Architecture during the January break.

Sample Good Essay 6: As an athlete, leader, and aspiring business executive, I want to major in Recreation Management, and Dreamschool College is one of the few private universities to offer this major as part of the Travel and Tourism Department. My dream is to open up a series of resort hotels that offer indoor skiing in tropical and subtropical climates. At Dreamschool, I could combine my studies of Recreation Management with a second major in Hotel Administration. I would also take courses in Landscape Architecture to learn how to plan recreational facilities—or at least to be able to read other people's plans—and Entrepreneurship and Business Management. I would enjoy the co-op program at Dreamschool, and would hope to gain some work experience at hotels and resorts during the course of my studies. And finally, having been captain of my high school's Downhill Ski Team, I would try out for the Dreamschool Ski Team as well, and I'd make use of the campus's many cross-country trails too.

Sample Good Essay 7: Ever since I started babysitting and working summers at a local day camp, I realized that what fascinated me was psychology—specifically child psychology. As an avid reader of *Psychology Today* and books by all of the famous child psychologists, I would find it very exciting to be able to study with Prof. Jane Smith, whose authoritative book, *Child and Teen Psychology,* I've read three times and quote frequently. Dreamschool's internships in inner-city day-care centers appeal to me particularly, because that would give me the opportunity to work with young children while giving back to the community. And I would likely opt for the Elementary Education Teaching Certificate Program, in case I choose to teach instead of becoming a psychologist.

Sample Good Essay 8: Having formed a Poetry Reading Club at my high school, I am hoping to major in English Literature at Dreamschool, which is one of the few Midwestern universities to offer a Poetry minor. I would be very excited to be able to take the course The Poetry of Shelley, and other courses focused exclusively on e.e. cummings, and T. S. Eliot. Nowhere else have I seen such specific courses. At Dreamschool, I would participate actively in the Poet's Corner Coffee House. In fact, I like to write poems, and I would read some of my own work and try to publish in the campus *Dreams Literary Magazine.* I would also enjoy exploring Linguistics and Philosophy, two subjects that are not offered at my high school, but about which I have read a lot. And I would like to try out for the Dreamschool Shakespeare Players as well.

Sample Good Essay 9: Chemistry has always been my passion, and I am hoping to major in Chemistry at Dreamschool. Having been a member of the winning team of the Center Town Science Bowl and having worked in a chemistry laboratory last summer and a local pharmacy part-time during the school year, I am eager to learn more chemistry for a possible career in pharmaceutical science. What I find especially appealing about Dreamschool's Chemistry major is the option to specialize in pharmacy-related chemistry. I definitely would plan to utilize this option. And I would also relish the opportunity to conduct original medical-related research in Dreamschool's Pharmacology Laboratories as part of the Undergraduate Research Institute Program.

Sample Good Essay 10: As one who hasn't decided specifically what I want to major in in college, what excites me most about Dreamschool are the multiple options for courses and internships within the fields of History, Political Science, Public Policy, and Urban Planning. As a very successful debater, I know that I want to go on to law school eventually, and I'd like to pursue a policy-related career that would allow me to serve the community and speak out for good causes. Any of these majors would be a good match. In History, I am very interested in Urban History and The World's Great Cities. In Political Science, I am most interested in Urban Politics, and Charismatic Leaders. In Public Policy, I'm captivated by such courses as Creating Responsive Public Institutions, Government Agencies and Economic Crises, and Public School Systems. And in Urban Planning, I'm fascinated by courses like Urban Infrastructure.

Notice that the essays you've just read point specifically to what programs appeal to each applicant. Think of this essay as if you're reading a menu of all the options available at a university and then writing up your choices for the waiter. You're asked to select the options that appeal to you most. It's that simple. Fancy language is not necessary—nor is an artsy approach. Just tell the college directly what it has that you want (and that fits in with your background so far). And if you don't find what you want, you know you're applying to the wrong college for you.

When parents of highly qualified students (students with high GPAs and high standardized test scores) phone me after Early Decision notifications have been sent out to tell me that their child was deferred or rejected from competitive universities that seemed within solid statistical range (in terms of GPAs and tests) and ask if I might evaluate the student's application retroactively to help them find reasons for the rejections, I generally go first to the Why Do You Want to Come Here? essay for answers. Many of the very top students do very badly on this essay, not meeting most of the scoring criteria. This essay often goes unchecked—English teachers and guidance counselors don't bother reviewing it with students, since it's "just a mini essay." Everyone is so focused on the main essay instead. And so many students write this essay haphazardly without checking out the offerings and opportunities of each college. Big mistake.

WORD AND CHARACTER LIMITS

When writing your own Why Do You Want to Come Here? essay, note that colleges generally allot little space for these essays. Colleges prefer short, to-the-point essays and often provide strict word or space limits. For most colleges, if there's a computer character or letter limit, the punctuation and spaces between words count as part of the character count. Before writing your essay, check the essay prompt to see if there is a character limit. (Often colleges will specify "including spaces" or "words only, not including spaces.") I have seen students confuse the word limit with the character limit and produce essays that are far too long.

BEFORE WRITING YOUR ESSAY, ASSEMBLE YOUR INFORMATION

When writing your essay, first write your prospective major (choosing a subject that meshes with your own high school track record and experiences) here:

Major _____

Next, list three enticing courses that the college offers in your prospective major:

1. _____

2. _____

3. _____

Next, make a list of at least two noncourse opportunities the college offers that directly relate to your prospective major here: (e.g., a program abroad, an interdepartmental project, field studies, research, internships).

1. _____

2. _____

Next, choose a few courses and programs outside your proposed major that interest you, as something new to explore. (Remember: Your essay will focus mostly on the area of interest that you're calling your major. But you might mention one or two of these additional courses or programs also toward the end of your mini essay.)

1. _____

2. _____

3. _____

Next, look over the campus activities, clubs, and volunteer opportunities to envision which ones you might choose for active involvement. List the clubs or activities by their exact names as they're listed at the college website (e.g., Dreamschool Chorus versus Dreamschool Choir versus Dreamers Glee Club).

1. _____

2. _____

3. _____

Now list any professors in your prospective major whose work you have read and under whose guidance you might enjoy doing research. If you're not familiar with any professors or their work, this might be an opportunity for the most ambitious students to look up some of the names and their work. This is particularly applicable for the most competitive colleges that offer extensive research programs. For most college applicants, this section does not apply. So it's okay to leave this blank.

1. _____

2. _____

3. _____

Finally, list any research that Dreamschool College is pursuing that especially appeals to you. Where do you find what research they're doing? The best place is usually at the website of the department in which you want to major. Go to that website and click "Faculty." Most colleges that have significant research offer bios of their professors, including descriptions of what research the professors are currently pursuing. You might cite one or two interesting projects in your essay. (If you are applying to a less competitive college or one that is not known for its research, you may leave this section blank.)

1. _____

2. _____

3. _____

Now using all of the names and resources you have listed, assemble this information into an essay. Remember to cite your track record—one or two of your best credentials that specially qualify you for the major you have chosen—to score extra points.

• WRITE YOUR ESSAY NOW •

Once you are finished writing your mini essay, use the scorecard at the beginning of this chapter to grade it. If you don't like your score, rework your essay to improve your score.

Describe Your Most Meaningful Activity Essay

The Common Application has asked in recent years that students *"briefly elaborate on one of your extracurricular activities or work experiences . . ."* in *"150 words or fewer."* While this is not meant to be a trick question, this is often the mini essay where colleges get to see who the candidate really is. It's helpful to the colleges to make sure that they have the facilities and resources to accommodate the applicant. If not, this could be a good reason to turn away the applicant (e.g., if you write that your favorite activity is weekend skiing and you're applying to a college in Florida, they know you won't be happy there, so they might easily turn you away, reasoning that they're doing this in your own best interests). In addition, this essay can provide a handy means of verifying the information on the rest of the application, since hidden truths and inconsistencies may be quickly revealed. The applicant, for example, who writes the main essay on her passion for medical research and how she's a motivated student, and then writes the Most Meaningful Activity essay on how she hates schoolwork but loves walking the dog, shopping, or video games, etc. FYI: I've seen at least five kids write about sleeping over the years. Although you may be tired, writing about sleeping is not a good idea.

Don't ignore this essay just because it's only 150 words. This little essay could be the make-or-break essay for admission depending on the college and the response that you write. Many students write off the essay as something trivial and miss out on a significant opportunity to strengthen their applications. For example, if you write that your most meaningful activity is your tuba playing, and the college doesn't have a band, you might be out. But if the college has been seeking tuba players for its tuba band, this may be the ticket to get in, even with a slightly lower GPA or standardized test scores than the rest of the college's preferred applicants. If your most meaningful activity is translating texts into Turkish, and the college is opening up a brand-new Turkish Department, you may suddenly be seen as a valuable student.

Make sure to focus this essay on one of the activities that you have listed on your application as a job, internship, or extra-curricular activity. Do not suddenly bring in unlisted activities like dog walking, beach walking, talking on the phone, shopping, etc.

Following are some short essays that illustrate the types of essays that students typically write. Each student is given a one- or two-word "reference name" (nickname) by our committee (shown in capital letters before their essay), as a means of remembering each one when it comes time to discuss them. You'll see that some essays and essay topics are much more helpful to the student than others. Once again, here's your chance to pretend to be an admissions officer. Grade the mini essays using the following criteria:

POINTS

ADD points for the following features:

- **Meaningful contribution:** Would the student's most meaningful activity contribute to the college in some meaningful or needed way? (30 points meaningful; 50 points needed)
- **Suitable activity:** Does the college offer a suitable activity or activities to meet this student's interests? (30 points)
- **Consistent interests:** Does the activity seem to back up everything the student said earlier in the application? Do the student's interests sound consistent? (Since you, the reader, are unable to read the rest of each student's application, we will credit the students who devote this essay to describing academic, artistic, athletic, or community service pursuits that we will presume they listed among their "most meaningful activities" on a previous page in the application.) (20 points)

1. GUITAR GIRL: Playing my guitar is the most meaningful activity to me. I can just sit and play for hours. I like to express myself, so I play a variety of songs depending on my moods. When I'm really happy, for example, I play old-fashioned Beach Boys. When I'm depressed, I fancy myself a blues singer, and I play some of the saddest blues imaginable. Sometimes I like to play in front of a mirror and imitate current pop stars like Madonna and Justin Timberlake. After playing the guitar, I'm ready to handle anything—including homework.

Points

- Meaningful contribution (30 or 50 points)   _____

- Suitable activity (30 points)   _____

- Consistent interests (20 points)   _____

                TOTAL   _____

2. INVENTOR: Last year, I invented a device that detects biological pollutants in a hospital room. This year, my inventions have focused more on a variety of braces that can be used in the healing process. My science research and medical inventions together comprise my most meaningful activity. One of my inventions has been awarded a patent, and nurses say they've already gotten much use out of my braces. Knowing that I'm helping people makes my love of inventing worthwhile.

Points

- Meaningful contribution (30 or 50 points)   _____

- Suitable activity (30 points)   _____

- Consistent interests (20 points)   _____

                TOTAL   _____

3. CROSS-COUNTRY SKIER: Cross-country skiing helps me stay in shape, takes me to new places and keeps me in good company, so I find it most meaningful. My family usually goes cross-country skiing in February at Mt. Tremblant, Canada, known for its incomparable trails. We pass waterfalls, and the trails are paved, have lanes, and are well marked with traffic signs warning of steep inclines. Cars are prohibited. The other foreign vacationers who we meet along the way tend to be very interesting.

Points

- Meaningful contribution (30 or 50 points)   _____
- Suitable activity (30 points)   _____
- Consistent interests (20 points)   _____

TOTAL   _____

4. GOURMET COOK: Cooking is the most meaningful activity to me, mainly because I have to eat, but also, because I come from a great cooking tradition. My dad is Italian and my mom is Hungarian, both cultures that are known for their hardy cuisine and generosity with food. I make the best goulash, and my lasagna can't be beat. Of course, my second most meaningful activity is dieting.

Points

- Meaningful contribution (30 or 50 points)   _____
- Suitable activity (30 points)   _____
- Consistent interests (20 points)   _____

TOTAL   _____

5. READER: My most meaningful activity is reading. I particularly like the classics. I read *Moby Dick,* for example, while on a family cruise. I read *Catcher in the Rye* while commuting by bus each to day work one summer. I read *The Old Man and the Sea* in one reading at a friend's beach house. And I read some Shakespeare on a study tour of London. I also like good movies, particularly films that are based on other cultures—in settings I would never otherwise really get to see.

                                                          Points

- Meaningful contribution (30 or 50 points)   _____
- Suitable activity (30 points)   _____
- Consistent interests (20 points)   _____

                              TOTAL   _____

6. TOPIARY MEDALIST: Running the school greenhouse is the most meaningful activity to me. Ever since I was one of four students to win the National Biology Olympiad, I've become newly obsessed with botany, specifically horticultural design. I am considering becoming a professional landscape architect—possibly for theme parks and public gardens. I seem to have a special talent for topiary. I have cut plants to look like elephants and donkeys on Election Day. I have created serpents and dragons. I am entering the Intel Science Talent Search this year with a project on The Psychology of Topiary.

	Points
• Meaningful contribution (30 or 50 points)	_____
• Suitable activity (30 points)	_____
• Consistent interests (20 points)	_____
TOTAL	_____

7. SUNTAN: I'm into tanning. My parents bought me a one-year membership to a tanning salon, and they didn't waste their money. When I'm tan, I look great and that makes me feel confident. I spend a lot of time there each winter perfecting my tan. There's nothing quite as relaxing, and I know that when I leave, I look good and healthy.

	Points
• Meaningful contribution (30 or 50 points)	_____
• Suitable activity (30 points)	_____
• Consistent interests (20 points)	_____
TOTAL	_____

8. TV POTATO: Don't tell anyone, but my favorite activity is un-
winding with reality TV. I love seeing stars stuck on remote islands, or shows where attractive people are selected for dates, or
fashion designers compete for the best outfit, or executives
compete for top-paying jobs. I learn a lot on these shows and
have a good sense of what to do and what not to do when going
for an interview.

	Points
• Meaningful contribution (30 or 50 points)	_____
• Suitable activity (30 points)	_____
• Consistent interests (20 points)	_____
TOTAL	_____

9. BRIDGE/POKER: When I have downtime, I love to play cards. I
play any kind of cards, and have a reputation as quite the bridge
and poker player. I imagine that when I'm in college, I'll be able
to entertain the whole dorm floor with my games, and I enjoy
teaching other people to play bridge as well. I especially want to
join the college Bridge Club and kick some butt.

	Points
• Meaningful contribution (30 or 50 points)	_____
• Suitable activity (30 points)	_____
• Consistent interests (20 points)	_____
TOTAL	_____

10. BALLERINA: When I was six, I performed in *Sleeping Beauty* in a holiday presentation, and since then I've found ballet to be most meaningful. I attend dance classes three days per week, exercising on the other days to stay in shape. I perform in dance competitions and have won the New York State Championship and the opportunity to attend state-funded ballet camp this summer at Saratoga. I want to dance with the Dreamschool Ballet Company.

                                                                          Points

- Meaningful contribution (30 or 50 points)   _____

- Suitable activity (30 points)   _____

- Consistent interests (20 points)   _____

                                                  TOTAL   _____

11. YOUTH CLUB: Volunteering at my church youth club is most meaningful. I help local kids who might otherwise get into trouble. I run basketball, Bingo and crafts. While it's not very intellectual, I know I'm helping others, and I'm getting some experience working with children in case I want to teach someday.

                                                                          Points

- Meaningful contribution (30 or 50 points)   _____

- Suitable activity (30 points)   _____

- Consistent interests (20 points)   _____

                                                  TOTAL   _____

12. DEBATER: Debate is what's most meaningful. I've been winning a series of county tournaments and am hoping to go on to States next month. My expertise is Lincoln-Douglas style debate. I enjoy that style, because participants take turns arguing each side of every issue—liberal and conservative. I often help younger students to formulate arguments. Debate leads to clear thinking on issues.

	Points
• Meaningful contribution (30 or 50 points)	_____
• Suitable activity (30 points)	_____
• Consistent interests (20 points)	_____
TOTAL	_____

13. DOG BUDDY: If I'm to be honest, I would have to tell you that I like spending time with my dog. Other students may write about how they find academic activities most meaningful. But they're being phony. I'm being real in telling you that what I find really relaxing is taking my dog, Winnifred, on a long walk. Our time together is simple. No talk. No heavy debates. No arguments.

	Points
• Meaningful contribution (30 or 50 points)	_____
• Suitable activity (30 points)	_____
• Consistent interests (20 points)	_____
TOTAL	_____

14. POET LYRICIST: Having my poetry published in professional literary journals has been a most exciting experience for me. *Po-M,* the national journal, has printed five of my poems this year. In addition, I write for my high school literary magazine, and have been actively involved in editing the publication. I particularly like rhymed verse about contemporary issues, and like to write song lyrics as well. I'm going to try to sell some song lyrics this year to pop singers.

                                                                    Points

- Meaningful contribution (30 or 50 points)   _____

- Suitable activity (30 points)   _____

- Consistent interests (20 points)   _____

                                    TOTAL   _____

15. EMT RESCUER: A man almost died of a heart attack last weekend in the bathtub, but my ambulance team arrived on time to save him. A pregnant woman fainted in a parking lot, and we rushed her to the hospital on time. Of all the extracurricular activities I do, my stint as a volunteer Emergency Medical Technician aide is the most meaningful, because I can actually count the number of lives I've saved. It's tough, but I want to volunteer for the college Ambulance Corps when I get there.

                                                                    Points

- Meaningful contribution (30 or 50 points)   _____

- Suitable activity (30 points)   _____

- Consistent interests (20 points)   _____

                                    TOTAL   _____

16. JOURNALIST: I'm a reporter for my high school newspaper and find journalism particularly rewarding. First of all, I find out what's going on in school before anyone else. In addition, reporting takes me to new places and forces me to meet new people. This is very good for me, since I tend to be shy and sedentary. I try to be fair and balanced, but I know I have trouble maintaining the pretense.

	Points
• Meaningful contribution (30 or 50 points)	_____
• Suitable activity (30 points)	_____
• Consistent interests (20 points)	_____
TOTAL	_____

17. SHOPPER: If the truth be known, I spend the majority of my spare time shopping. I know I'm supposed to write on this application that I read in my spare time, but truthfully, I find clothing shopping very meaningful and yes, challenging. It's important for a future lawyer to "look the part," and "dress for success." I have the wardrobe. Now all I need is the knowledge.

	Points
• Meaningful contribution (30 or 50 points)	_____
• Suitable activity (30 points)	_____
• Consistent interests (20 points)	_____
TOTAL	_____

18. BEACH WALKER: I like to clear my head by walking on the beach. There is nothing so refreshing as walking on the boardwalk near my home and smelling the nice ocean air. The boardwalk is exactly two miles long, so I usually take a full four-mile walk. And when I return home, I feel fully refreshed and ready to pursue a full night of studying.

	Points
• Meaningful contribution (30 or 50 points)	_____
• Suitable activity (30 points)	_____
• Consistent interests (20 points)	_____
TOTAL	_____

19. BASSOONIST: Practicing the bassoon is my favorite way to relax. The shelves in my bedroom are covered with reeds—I'm always preparing reeds so that I can practice often. I enjoy the fact that the bassoonists are relatively rare, and playing this instrument has taken me to the state orchestra. I am hoping to play in a good college orchestra.

	Points
• Meaningful contribution (30 or 50 points)	_____
• Suitable activity (30 points)	_____
• Consistent interests (20 points)	_____
TOTAL	_____

20. BAKER: I find baking to be a meaningful activity and plan to bake for the whole dorm someday in college. Although I want to major in German Literature, I'm sure I'll find a dorm kitchen where I can bake and decorate cookies, especially for the holidays. Nothing is better for a night of studying than a plate of warm chocolate chip cookies, fresh out of the oven.

	Points
• Meaningful contribution (30 or 50 points)	_____
• Suitable activity (30 points)	_____
• Consistent interests (20 points)	_____
TOTAL	_____

YOUR CHOICES

If you were on the Admissions Committee for one of the most competitive colleges in the United States, you would be asked to select two students out of the 20 essays. The rest would be deferred or declined admission. Based on the points you've assigned to each essay, which two would you accept? Don't be surprised if you have trouble deciding among the top scorers!

1. _____

2. _____

Who would be your third and fourth choice if you were on the committee at a school that admitted 15 percent or 20 percent?

3. _____

4. _____

Now see how your evaluations compare to the author's.

HOW THE "MOST MEANINGFUL" ACTIVITIES ESSAYS COMPARE

1. GUITARIST		Points	Explanation
• Meaningful contribution (30 or 50 points)		0	*If the author offers to play in a college band, we might award more points. But there's no mention of how well he/she plays)*
• Suitable activity	(30 points)	0	
• Consistent interests	(20 points)	0	*Doesn't tie this in with any major or subject*
	FINAL SCORE:	0	

2. INVENTOR		Points	Explanation
• Meaningful contribution (30 or 50 points)		50	*This sounds like a student who will appreciate what our university offers, and likely contribute to the college environment.*
• Suitable activity	(30 points)	30	*We likely have labs to accommodate this student's interests*
• Consistent interests	(20 points)	20	*Likely consistent with the rest of the student's application*
	FINAL SCORE:	100	

3. CROSS-COUNTRY SKIER		Points	Explanation
• Meaningful contribution	(30 or 50 points)	0	*But if we need new ski-team members, this candidate's points could go up significantly*
• Suitable activity	(30 points)	30	*Assuming the college is located in a region that gets winter snow or has access to snow*
• Consistent interests	(20 points)	0	
	FINAL SCORE:	30	

4. GOURMET		Points	Explanation
• Meaningful contribution	(30 or 50 points)	0	
• Suitable activity	(30 points)	0	
• Consistent interests	(20 points)	0	
	FINAL SCORE:	0	

5. READER		Points	Explanation
• Meaningful contribution (30 or 50 points)		0	*While our college loves readers and loves to fill our classes with readers, we're not so impressed that this student is an outstanding reader. All the books mentioned are within standard American high school repertoire — nothing exceptional. And our college has many English majors, so we don't see anything unique that this candidate presents. We've seen applications by students who have claimed to read more than 100 books in the past year, including many foreign authors who aren't included in the standard American high school curriculum. That impresses us much more.*
• Suitable activity	(30 points)	30	*Assuming the college has book clubs and film nights*
• Consistent interests	(20 points)	20	*Likely the applicant expressed an interest in literature or film in main application essay*
	FINAL SCORE:	**50**	

6. TOPIARY MEDALIST		Points	Explanation
• Meaningful contribution	(30 or 50 points)	30–50	*Depending on our need for botany majors or greenhouse enthusiasts, and depending if our college offers Landscape Architecture*
• Suitable activity	(30 points)	30	*Assuming our college has a greenhouse*
• Consistent interests	(20 points)	20	*Assuming the applicant wrote about his/her interest in biology for the main application*
	FINAL SCORE:	**80–100**	

7. SUNTAN		Points	Explanation
• Meaningful contribution	(30 or 50 points)	0	
• Suitable activity	(30 points)	0	
• Consistent interests	(20 points)	0	
	FINAL SCORE:	**0**	

8. TV POTATO		Points	Explanation
• Meaningful contribution	(30 or 50 points)	0	
• Suitable activity	(30 points)	0	
• Consistent interests	(20 points)	0	
	FINAL SCORE:	**0**	

9. BRIDGE/POKER		Points	Explanation
• Meaningful contribution (30 or 50 points)		0	*Assuming the Bridge Club isn't lacking members*
• Suitable activity	(30 points)	30	
• Consistent interests	(20 points)	0	*Unrelated to an academic interest*
	FINAL SCORE:	**30**	

10. BALLERINA		Points	Explanation
• Meaningful contribution (30 or 50 points)		50	*Assuming the college ballet company needs an award-winning dancer*
• Suitable activity	(30 points)	30	
• Consistent interests	(20 points)	20	
	FINAL SCORE:	**100**	

11. YOUTH CLUB		Points	Explanation
• Meaningful contribution (30 or 50 points)		30	*Meaningful, but not necessarily specially needed by the college*
• Suitable activity	(30 points)	30	*Most colleges offer local tutoring*
• Consistent interests	(20 points)	10	*Relevant to a possible teaching career*
	FINAL SCORE:	**100**	

12. DEBATER		Points	Explanation
• Meaningful contribution (30 or 50 points)		30	*Meaningful, but not necessarily needed*
• Suitable activity	(30 points)	30	*Assuming we offer a debate team*
• Consistent interests	(20 points)	10	*Not necessarily an extension of an academic, artistic, athletic or community service interest*
	FINAL SCORE:	**70**	

13. DOG BUDDY		Points	Explanation
• Meaningful contribution (30 or 50 points)		0	
• Suitable activity	(30 points)	0	
• Consistent interests	(20 points)	0	
	FINAL SCORE:	**0**	

14. POET LYRICIST		Points	Explanation
• Meaningful contribution (30 or 50 points)		50	*Meaningful to have a published poet as part of the student body to help staff the college literary journal*
• Suitable activity	(30 points)	30	
• Consistent interests	(20 points)	20	*Likely to be consistent with the rest of the student's application essays*
	FINAL SCORE:	**100**	

15. EMT RESCUER		Points	Explanation
• Meaningful contribution (30 or 50 points)		50	*Meaningful and needed*
• Suitable activity	(30 points)	30	
• Consistent interests	(20 points)	20	
	FINAL SCORE:	**100**	

16. JOURNALIST		Points	Explanation
• Meaningful contribution (30 or 50 points)		30	
• Suitable activity	(30 points)	30	
• Consistent interests	(20 points)	10	*Assuming some interest in a journalism major, which the applicant doesn't state*
	FINAL SCORE:	**70**	

17. SHOPPER		Points	Explanation
• Meaningful contribution (30 or 50 points)		0	
• Suitable activity	(30 points)	0	
• Consistent interests	(20 points)	0	
	FINAL SCORE:	**0**	

18. BEACH WALKER		Points	Explanation
• Meaningful contribution	(30 or 50 points)	0	
• Suitable activity	(30 points)	0	
• Consistent interests	(20 points)	0	
	FINAL SCORE:	**0**	

19. BASSOONIST		Points	Explanation
• Meaningful contribution	(30 or 50 points)	50	*Good bassoonists are rare and needed*
• Suitable activity	(30 points)	30	
• Consistent interests	(20 points)	0–20	*If the applicant is really good on the bassoon to be determined by audition*
	FINAL SCORE:	**80–100**	

20. BAKER		Points	Explanation
• Meaningful contribution	(30 or 50 points)	0	
• Suitable activity	(30 points)	0	
• Consistent interests	(20 points)	0	
	FINAL SCORE:	**0**	

WHO GETS IN?

Surely you've noticed that the rubric or scorecard used in this chapter is much simpler than the previous scorecards. But also notice that the scores are still far apart, ranging from eight students who received zeros, to five students who were in the range of 100s.

While this essay is rarely the sole determining factor of an application, a borderline candidate with a 100 is likely to get in, whereas a borderline candidate with a low score or zero is likely to get pushed out by another applicant who shows more enthusiasm for academic pursuits, or the arts, unique athletics, or community service opportunities that the college offers. Notice that the students with the zeroes are also the students who focused their essays on hobbies or pastimes that don't really contribute in any way to the academic, athletic, artistic, or community service environment of the college: a casual guitar player, a gourmet, a sun tanner, a TV potato, a dog buddy, a shopper, and a baker. While these pursuits may indeed be worthwhile, relaxing, and appealing to many people, these aren't the students we're eager to get at Dreamschool, if we're only allowed to accept a limited number of students.

Top on our list are EMT Rescuer, Poet Lyricist, Inventor, Bassoonist, Ballerina, and Topiary Medalist—all people with very different interests and backgrounds. Next on our list would be Youth Club, Debater, Journalist, and then Reader. The Journalist is irritating, implying that being "fair and balanced" is a pretense, so admissions committee members lobby against him. The Reader might have been more interesting if she had told us which Shakespeares she had read, or if she cited books that weren't contained in the traditional high school curriculum, demonstrating to us that she really *does* read beyond school assignments.

While other applicants like the Dog Buddy or the Baker might be perfectly wonderful human beings, we're limited in space at Dreamschool, and they haven't used this essay opportunity to present a compelling argument for us to accept them. In fact, they've squandered this chance.

Describe an Issue and Its Importance to You

The Common Application gives you five choices for your main essay, plus a sixth option of an open-ended essay on the "topic of your choice." As mentioned earlier in this book, I generally recommend that students choose Option 1: *Evaluate a significant experience, achievement, risk you have taken, or ethical dilemma you have faced and its impact on you.* But some students—especially students involved in environmental work or students involved in helping to resolve other issues—prefer to devote the main essay to describing this involvement. For such issue-involved students, Option 2 is an excellent choice: *Discuss some issue of personal, local, national, or international concern and its importance to you.* For students who are not involved in social action, volunteering, or politics, I again recommend electing Option 1 instead.

In responding to Option 2, the second half of the question—"its importance to you"—is the most crucial part, since ultimately the college admissions officers use this essay to learn more about *you,* rather than wanting to learn more about the issue you're discussing. If you choose to respond to this essay, make sure you understand that your main mission is not to educate the admissions officers about politics, but rather to tell them who you are.

Also, most of the same rules (and point system) apply to the main essay described in Chapter 2. Your "issues" essay should also mention your track record, suitable program, contribution and diversity, and focus—the same elements discussed in Chapter 2.

TIP 1: The most common error in responding to this essay is for the student to leave him- or herself out of the essay entirely and to focus solely on the issue being discussed, as if the applicant is writing a third-person paper on history, government, environmental science, or economics for a social studies course.

TIP 2: Choose your issues wisely. Be wary about choosing topics that are so controversial or unpopular that you might end up alienating the admissions officers entirely. Yes, many admissions officers claim to be open-minded, and they want your "true voice" to come through. But be smart and take that with a grain of salt. Advocating crime, substance abuse, or violence will never get you admitted. If you have very unpopular viewpoints and perspectives, the college application isn't the best time to share them, even if your parents think your offbeat views are adorable, or if they roll their eyes and say, "you're just acting like a typical teenager," and even if you think that the college you are applying to has very "liberal" views and will understand. Colleges don't have views. Applications are read by individual admissions officers who are a diverse group. You never know who is reading your application and what his or her views are.

TIP 3: In writing this essay, you need to propose solutions—not just problems. Having ideas for solutions demonstrates that you've taken the time to think through the issue—that it's genuinely important to you. In addition, to make the essay stronger, you need to tell the reader what *you* are doing about the issue. Many students only talk about what *other people ought to do* about the problem. That sounds passive and lazy, and doesn't make you sound like an appealing candidate.

TIP 4: Watch the way you present yourself in this essay in terms of your emotions. Don't make yourself out to be angry, hostile, unreasonable, frustrated, depressed, or stymied. Remember that the admissions committee isn't reading this essay to learn more about the cause—instead, they're reading it to find out more about *you.* How you present yourself and your responses is paramount.

TIP 5: Avoid topics that rely heavily on religion or politics, especially where admissions officers are likely to disagree. Do not just repeat the rhetoric that you hear from others.

TIP 6: Although it may be very tempting, the issue essay isn't the place to air your school's or family's dirty laundry or to bad-mouth anyone. Don't use this essay to tattle on your school or family. In 95 percent of the cases, speaking ill of your school or family will backfire on you and make you look bad to colleges. No colleges want complainers or whiners, even if the cause is somewhat noble.

TIP 7: While I generally recommend a "happy ending," moral, or conclusion for main essays, this "issue" essay needs an extra-happy or upbeat ending. You don't want to end on a sour or despairing note. The happy ending could be that you plan to study this topic further in college to be able to do more about it as part of your long-term career. College admissions officers (and most other people as well) are much more attracted to energetic optimists than depressed pessimists. Your ending cannot be a "call to action" for the admissions committee. They are administrators, not activists.

For this essay, we'll use a slightly different scorecard than the one used for the Chapter 2 "Evaluate a significant experience" essay, changing some of the categories. In addition to 1) Track Record, 2) Suitable Program, 3) Contribution and Diversity, and 4) Focus, we'll add:

5) Clearly stating the chosen issue (colleges want to make sure that you understand the issue, and they want to understand the issue as well).

6) Relating the issue to the applicant (the prompt asks you to discuss the issue's "importance to you," so you need to mention how you are related to or involved personally with the issue).

7) Offering a viable solution that's not overly simplistic (it's not enough to just complain about a problem—colleges want to see what thinking and recommendations you have to offer that show genuine concern. And the solution needs to be viable, meaning you can't offer a solution of "wishing away a problem" or "finding funding," without specifying how or where).

8) Showing the student's own response (colleges are very attracted to students who try to respond actively by doing something concrete to help settle the issue or remedy the problem, rather than just talking).

In addition, 50 points will be subtracted for an offensive view—one that offends the admissions officer reading your application, or advocates crime or violence, religious conversion, hatred, or discrimination.

HANDY SCORECARD
(for main "issue" essay)

ADD points for the following:

1. Track Record   (20 points)
2. Suitable Program   (15 points)
3. Contribution & Diversity   (15 points)
4. Focus   (10 points)
5. Clearly Stated Issue   (15 points)
6. Relating the Issue   (5 points)
7. Viable Solution   (10 points)
8. Student's Response   (10 points)

SUBTRACT points for the following:

1. Sloppiness/Carelessness   (20 points)
2. Inaccuracy   (20 points)
3. Bias   (20 points)
4. Offensive View   (50 points)

The most successful essays show that you are proactive about the issue you claim to care most about. The least successful essays talk about what should be done about the issue by others, without even offering a viable course of action or any involvement on your part. Note that the topics vary for this essay; there's no one topic that wins admission. There's no one political leaning that wins admission either. Many students lose significant points by failing to show a track record of how the issue they chose to discuss relates to their own background and experience. And the biggest point losers are the essays that contain bias.

REMINDER: In writing the issue essay, remember that the essay is most of all about who you are and why colleges should accept you. That should be the primary focus. The issue that you're discussing is merely a platform for you to provide this information.

WRITING YOUR ISSUE ESSAY

Now it's your turn. Follow the steps below.

STEP 1: Copy the list you made in Chapter 3 of your best credentials:

1. _____

2. _____

3. _____

STEP 2: Write the college major that best ties in with these credentials.

_____

STEP 3: Now write your issue (make sure it relates to your credentials listed above and your prospective major as listed above):

My issue is: _____

STEP 4: Now write your position on that issue:

My position is that: _____

SAMPLE FOR JESSICA JAMES

STEP 1: Three Best Credentials:

1. I did an internship at Central Nature Preserve and led children's wildlife programs there.

2. I organized a Central County Beach cleanup in which 200 people participated.

3. I helped build a coastal trail at Kenai Fjords National Park in Alaska as a high school crew member of the Student Conservation Association.

STEP 2: Major: Environmental Engineering

STEP 3: My issue is whether or not the county should permit energy-producing windmills to be built along the public beach.

STEP 4: My position is that even though some people think that windmills are not attractive, windmills are good for the environment and should be built along the shore.

Issue Essay Structure

PARAGRAPH 1: Start the essay like a novel in first or third person; then state the conflict.

PARAGRAPH 2: Who, what, when, where, why, how

PARAGRAPHS 3 AND 4: State your position and best credentials

PARAGRAPH 5: Your personal resolution

THE FIRST PARAGRAPH: Start the essay as if you're starting a great story. Use a first- or third-person description. Then state the conflict.

Sample first paragraph: The cool powdery sand glistened in the sunlight as if it were preparing for the next season of tourists. The white granules provided a spectacular contrast to the roaring blue ocean, the cloudless blue sky, and the bright red flowers planted nearby. Looking off into the distance to see if I could see any ships approaching, I suddenly spotted them—10 new giant windmills, hard at work, just off the coast. The newspaper editorials had warned that these "monstrosities" would destroy the serenity of the beach and the perfect view, but I saw beauty in these energy-saving monsters.

THE SECOND PARAGRAPH: In this paragraph, you should provide the details of the issue—the who, what, when, where, why, how. What makes this an issue now? And what's the scope of the issue? Is it national? International? Local?

Sample second paragraph: The issue of whether to build a series of 50 windmills just off the coast was hotly disputed in Central County two years ago. Hundreds of residents came to meetings of the Central County Coastal Authority to try to block the construction of the mills. But hundreds of others supported the measure. Energy officials felt strongly that the new structures would save taxpayers millions of dollars and that the windmills were far more energy efficient and responsible for a coastal county such as ours. So the county ultimately decided to go ahead with the construction, which was just completed this past spring.

THE THIRD AND FOURTH PARAGRAPHS: State your position and your best credentials (the credentials that you listed above). Tell the Admissions Committee everything you most want them to know about you here.

Sample third and fourth paragraphs: I was a proponent of the new windmills right from the start. In fact, I have always been an advocate of harnessing wind energy and solar energy as a means of preserving our planet's natural resources. So during the county dispute, when the discussions first started, I wrote an opinion piece for my school newspaper in an attempt to win more support for the windmills, and that article was reprinted in the town newspaper and discussed throughout the county. But that wasn't the first time I played a leadership role as an environmental activist.

Two summers ago, just before the windmills became an issue, I was working as an intern at Central Nature Preserve. There, I led children's wildlife programs—introducing children to snakes, lizards, and turtles— and in my talks, I emphasized my love of wildlife and the importance of recycling. Then last summer, I helped build a coastal trail at Kenai Fjords National Park in Alaska, as part of a Student Conservation Association high school crew. There, I learned about protecting the wildlife and saving energy. Then this past September, I organized a Central County Beach cleanup in which 200 people participated. We coordinated our efforts with the Ocean Conservancy's International Coastal Cleanup Day, and collected bottles, cans and hundreds of pounds of garbage. I realized that garbage and dumping are the real threats to our oceans, not windmills.

THE FIFTH PARAGRAPH: This should provide your resolution— how you grew from the experience and how this influenced or impacted you. Also tie up any loose ends, and end on an upbeat note.

Sample fifth paragraph: Two years after the dispute died down, I look off into the distance on a glorious spring day at the beach and see ten of the once-maligned windmills faithfully churning away, saving money for the local residents and resources for the planet. No one complains that the beach has been destroyed. In fact, to me these hard workers look mighty and regal. And they inspire me to pursue my dream of studying environmental engineering in college.

Describe a Person, Character, or Artwork with Significant Influence on You

In the Common Application, Personal Essay prompts 3 and 4 are basically the same question: Discuss a person (real or fictional) or work of art that has influenced you—and how that person or work has influenced you. To be more specific, Option 3 asks the applicant to "*Indicate a person who has had a significant influence on you, and describe that influence.*" Option 4 asks the applicant to "*Describe a character in fiction, a historical figure, or a creative work (as in art, music, science, etc.) that has had an influence on you, and explain that influence.*"

In both essays, the most important part of the prompt—the part that colleges care about most—is the second part, how you were influenced. After all, the purpose of having you write these essays is to allow the colleges to find out more about *you*, rather than the person or work you are describing. You might write about George Washington or your grandmother, but *they* are not applying to college, so you don't want the essay to focus too much on them.

I have read beautiful essays: one comes to mind in particular—about a grandfather who rescued people from the Nazis during World War II. After reading the essay, I was more than sold on accepting the grandfather, but I felt I had not learned much about the grandson. He barely mentioned himself.

The biggest mistake that most applicants make in writing these essays is devoting far too much space to describing the person or artwork, and far too little space discussing how that person or artwork influenced who the applicant is today. In fact, many applicants inadvertently omit any discussion of how they were influenced, devoting the entire essay to describing the person or work. Bad mistake. This is your big opportunity to tell the admissions office why they should accept you. Don't forget to give them the reasons in your essay!

Start this essay by choosing a topic, as you would for the "experience essay" (described in Chapter 4). No, you don't need to go back there to read that chapter. Here's the gist.

Time to Choose Your Topic
(for Essay Prompts 3 & 4)

STEP 1: Figure out what subject you're likely to want to major in at the college of your choice. The strongest essays are the ones that tie in to and reveal your interests. Go to the college's website, and look at Academics and then Majors or Departments. Select the major that you think is best suited to the experiences you have had so far. (Yes, most colleges insist that you don't have to select your major in advance, but play along for now. If you can't decide between two majors that you love equally and in which you have a track record already, choose the one that you think most people won't choose—your odds will be better much of the time.)

Write the major here: _____.

Make sure you write the name of the major exactly as the university writes it. If the university calls the subject Political Science instead of Government, then you too should call it Political Science in your application.

STEP 2: Make a list of your five *best* (unique) reasons, credentials, or accomplishments for *that* major. (If you can't think of any, then go back and find a more suitable major.)

Only use recent (high-school-age) credentials—nothing from elementary school days or even middle school days, unless it's a national- or international-level credential. Sample national- or international-level credentials: Speaking at a national rally in Washington, having a speaking role in a Hollywood film, performing an instrumental solo at Carnegie Hall, competing in the Olympics or Junior Olympics, winning the National Spelling Bee, winning the Intel Science Talent Search, writing an article that's published in a national publication (*The New York Times, Time* magazine, etc.), having your artwork exhibited at a nationally known museum, dancing in *The Nutcracker* with a professional ballet company, soloing with a major opera company, starring on Broadway, earning a patent for an original invention, saving a life, raising an inordinate amount of money for a major charity ($10,000+). Nobody on the admissions committee wants to read essays about how you were the first to learn to read in nursery school, or how cute you looked when you won the starring role at age five in the ballet school performance.

List your reasons, credentials, and related accomplishments here:

1. _____

2. _____

3. _____

4. _____

5. _____

SAMPLE: Jacob Johnson wants to apply to be a Library Science major at Random University.

JACOB'S FIVE MOST-RELATED CREDENTIALS

1. Jacob took a summer course in Library Science at nearby Central Community College.

2. Jacob was president of the School Book Discussion Club at high school.

3. Jacob organized a reading tutoring program for financially underprivileged children.

4. Jacob worked at the local library after school.

5. Jacob invited a local author to speak at his school.

SAMPLE: Emily Michaels wants to be a Chemistry and Pre-Pharmacy major at Random University.

EMILY'S FIVE MOST-RELATED CREDENTIALS

1. Emily won a Chemistry Prize in the Central Regional Science Fair.

2. Emily volunteers once a week to tutor younger students in Chemistry.

3. Emily organized a fund-raiser to buy new Bunsen burners for her high school.

4. Emily worked as an intern at a local pharmacy.

5. Emily took a summer course on Chemistry at nearby Central Community College.

STEP 3: Using the major that you've listed and each of the five credentials that you've listed, think of the personal stories and anecdotes that you associate with each of those five credentials. Make a list of five possible interesting true stories from your life—one for each credential that you've listed—that illustrate your interest or skill in *that* major. Along with each story subject, write who or what (artwork) influenced you and if any quotations are related.

Story 1: _____

Inspiration: _____

_____

Story 2: _____

Inspiration: _____

_____

Story 3: _____

     Inspiration: _____

                _____

Story 4: _____

     Inspiration: _____

                _____

Story 5: _____

     Inspiration: _____

                _____

SAMPLE FOR JACOB (BASED ON THE FIVE CREDENTIALS HE LISTED)

1. How Jacob gave a presentation on computer research to his college class at Central Community College.

Inspiration: Quotation from library science textbook chapter on computers

2. Resolving the heated discussion on Samuel Beckett at the school Book Discussion Club

Inspiration: Quotation from Beckett's play *Waiting for Godot*

3. How Jacob brought Dr. Seuss books into the reading tutoring program

Inspiration: Seuss quote: "The more that you read, the more things you will know. The more that you learn, the more places you'll go."

4. The time that Jacob was asked to create a display sign for a new sculpture at the library

Inspiration (work of art): The new sculpture

5. The time Jacob met author Joe Jolson at the library and invited him to speak at school

Inspiration: Quotation from Joe Jolson

SAMPLE FOR EMILY (BASED ON THE FIVE CREDENTIALS SHE LISTED):

1. Creating an original chemistry experiment that won First Prize

Inspiration: Quotation from the contest judge's speech upon awarding the prize

2. Highlights of teaching children Chemistry

Inspiration: Quotation of question asked by one of the children, and how that child's question influenced Emily's thinking

3. The hard work required in organizing a successful fundraiser

Inspiration: Emily's grandfather, who always quoted General Patton as saying: "Do more than is required of you."

4. The time a famous chemist came into the pharmacy

Inspiration: Quotation from famous chemist

5. The best chemistry demonstration (as a work of art) at Central Community College

Inspiration: Description of the inspiring demonstration

Most of the best essays—with the best real-world interactions and quotations—emerge from volunteering, internships, research, jobs, or creating an original work. In other words, engaging stories about something *positive* you've actively 1) done, 2) accomplished, or 3) experienced, and being able to tell the reader how you did what you did—that's what makes the strongest essays.

STEP 4: **From the five episodes (anecdotes and stories) that you've listed,** choose the one that you enjoy telling most—or the one that presents you in the best light. Most likely both will point to the same essay topic. That's your essay topic. Write it here:

Essay topic: _____

Inspiration: _____

STEP 5: Keep the remaining four topics handy. You will probably want to refer to them in the fourth paragraph of your essay where you mention your other related credentials. But you'll find out more about this later on in the chapter.

STEP 6: If you can't think of a person or work of art that inspired your best stories and anecdotes, then you'll probably find it easier to relay them purely as significant experiences or achievements (go back to Chapter 4 instead of this chapter). But if you're able to come up with related quotations, people, characters, or works of art, stay with this chapter. Is there something that someone said to you or that you read (a quotation) that impacted this story? If so, you'll want to start your essay with that quotation. Is there some work of art that inspired or impacted this story? If so, you'll want to describe that work of art and its influence at the beginning of your essay.

ALTERNATIVE APPROACH (*SKIP THIS SECTION IF YOU ALREADY HAVE YOUR TOPIC.*)

(What if You Have No Idea What You Want to Study or Have No Credentials?)

While it's usually better to have some idea of what you'd like to study, not everyone does. And not everybody arrives at senior year with a solid list of appealing credentials. You can still write a strong essay for Options 3 and 4, even if you have no clue as to what your dream major might be. But you'll still need to think of the five achievements of which you are most proud. If you didn't win any awards, you might list some different ways in which you've helped people or enlightened yourself (for example, volunteering as a tutor, working at a job after school to help the family meet its budget, farm chores, singing in the church choir, helping to organize a food drive, shoveling a neighbor's snow, pet-sitting, reading a series of books to gain expertise, or spending hours practicing a musical instrument—these too are achievements).

TO START: Make a list of five of your best credentials, talents, or achievements that you want to be sure to tell the admissions office—before you even look at the essay question. If you have trouble coming up with five items, ask your family members to help you think of five of your best qualities, achievements, or credentials.

The five qualities should *not* be adjectives. In other words, you don't want to list:

1. I'm sociable

2. I'm thoughtful

3. I'm creative

4. I'm responsible

5. I'm athletic

Instead, the five qualities should tell the admissions officers about the greatest things you *did* or *accomplished* in the last four or so years. This is the "message" you want to give the admissions committee somewhere in your essay.

SAMPLE ACCOMPLISHMENTS

1. I helped organize a fund-raising fashion show at school to raise money for a neighborhood boy who had cancer, and we managed to collect $1,200.

2. Every weekend I visit the senior citizen home nearby to spend time with some of the residents who don't get any other visitors.

3. My painting from art class was exhibited at the local library.

4. At the local bookstore where I work after school, I was given a certificate from the manager for being the only one to show up during the blizzard.

5. As a result of my archery record, I was named captain of the varsity team.

List your five credentials here:

Credential 1: _____

Credential 2: _____

Credential 3: _____

Credential 4: _____

Credential 5: _____

NEXT STEP: Using each of the five credentials that you've listed, think of the personal stories and anecdotes that you associate with those five credentials. Make a list of five related interesting stories. And with each story, consider who or what (artwork) influenced you or inspired you.

Story 1: _____

    Inspiration: _____

Story 2: _____

    Inspiration: _____

Story 3: _____

    Inspiration: _____

Story 4: _____

    Inspiration: _____

Story 5: _____

    Inspiration: _____

SAMPLE STORIES *(based on the sample accomplishments listed above):*

1. At the fund-raising fashion show, the principal got onstage to announce that this was the most thoughtful school event ever, and that a record amount of money was raised.

    Inspiration: Fashion designer Joan Latif, who said, "The fashion industry has always been very generous when it comes to donating to good causes."

2. At the senior home, one of the residents told me how he escaped from a concentration camp during World War II, and I developed an interest in wartime history.

Inspiration: Veteran John Smith of the Central Senior Home

3. Try to draw a pineapple—that was the assignment the teacher gave when my painting was ultimately selected for the local library exhibit.

Inspiration (work of art): Drawing of a pineapple

4. How I got to work the day of the blizzard

Inspiration: A great work of literature on Books on Tape in the car

5. The day the famous Olympic archer came to my archery class and offered me some personal tips on improving my aim

Inspiration: Quotation from the famous Olympic archer

NEXT STEP: From the five episodes (anecdotes and stories) that you've listed, choose the one that you enjoy telling most, or the one that presents you in the best light. Most likely both will point to the same essay topic. That's your essay topic.

TIP 1: If you ultimately decide to write your essay about a person, only write about a person with whom you feel thoroughly familiar. Do not write an essay, for example, based on what your parents or grandparents have told you about your great grandparents. In the end, your parents will want editorial control—I've seen it happen in so many families. They will want to make sure you are telling the family story correctly, and they'll end up writing the essay for you, or editing it so severely that you won't recognize any of your thoughts or wording in the essay. Instead, write your essay about a person or work of art that you feel personally familiar with.

TIP 2: If you choose to base your essay on a character in fiction, make sure the character is viewed intelligently and positively. Avoid writing a negative essay or an essay that belittles you. No essays on children's book characters (that indicate that you're still clinging to a low reading level), or cartoon characters (that indicate that you still enjoy kiddie entertainment). The exception would be if you plan to major in Children's Literature or Animation, and if you clearly state that in your essay.

TIP 3: If you are going to use a quotation to start, make sure the quotation somehow relates to the credentials you most want to tell the admissions officers about yourself. Keep your topic in mind when you choose the quotation.

TIP 4: If you're going to base your essay on an artistic work, make sure that the work is genuinely considered artistic. Choosing a TV ad is not considered art (unless you plan to major in Media Advertising and state that clearly in your essay). Choosing a current hit tune, or the drawing on a cereal box, or a TV sitcom, or the poetry inside a greeting card is not advised.

THE STRUCTURE OF THE PERSON/ARTWORK ESSAY

Option 1 (Quotation beginning)

PARAGRAPH 1: Exact quotation, attribution (who said the quote), and a sentence telling how the quotation relates to you

PARAGRAPH 2: Follow up more about how you've applied the quotation

PARAGRAPH 3 AND 4: Continue the story or anecdote; insert your strongest credentials

PARAGRAPH 5: Upbeat ending tying in the person with your story

OPTION 1: In the first paragraph, start with a quotation by the person you are writing about, and identify him or her. Also mention how the quotation relates to you in this first paragraph. Then the second paragraph follows up.

EXAMPLE 1 (QUOTATION BEGINNING)

First paragraph: "Be the change you want to see in the world." That was the philosophy of Mahatma Gandhi that inspired me to become involved in community action.

Second paragraph: Attempting to follow in Gandhi's tradition, I thought long and hard about what changes I most wanted to see in the world. I decided that the most immediate change needed to be feeding the hungry. So I first volunteered at a local soup kitchen to familiarize myself with the severity of the problem domestically and the current remedies.

EXAMPLE 2 (QUOTATION BEGINNING)

First paragraph: "Unless you try to do something beyond what you have already mastered, you will never grow." Ralph Waldo Emerson's words serve as a daily inspiration for me to challenge myself intellectually.

Second paragraph: In fact, Emerson's words were what encouraged me to enroll in AP Physics C. Having already taken Honors Physics and AP Calculus BC, I was initially intimidated by the more advanced Physics class. But I thoroughly enjoyed Honors Physics and became curious to learn more and grow further.

OPTION 2: In the first paragraph, start with a description of what the most influential person did that impressed you, or tell about the most engaging aspects of the work of art you decided to write about (instead of using a quotation). Use first or third person, as if you were writing a story or novel. Go right to the most exciting element first to draw the reader in. If you use Option 2, you can wait until the second paragraph to reveal your connection to the person or artwork.

Option 2 Description Beginning

PARAGRAPH 1: Description of the person or artwork in first or third person

PARAGRAPH 2: Your relationship to this person or artwork

PARAGRAPH 3: Continue the story

PARAGRAPH 4: Insert your credentials

PARAGRAPH 5: The happy ending, emphasizing how this person or artwork has influenced you.

FIRST PARAGRAPH: Describe the person or work of art, starting with the most dramatic or engaging aspect of the person or artwork you're describing.

EXAMPLE 1 (WORK OF ART BEGINNING)

First paragraph: Gunshots rang out. Bar fights ensued. At first, it seemed like a cheap Western with stereotypical cowboys and outdated depictions of the romance and glamour of the Wild West. The old Paul Newman film *Hombre* is not generally remembered as one of his most noteworthy political statements, and relatively few people are familiar with the movie.

Second paragraph (showing your connection to the film and what made it influential): But being the Newman fan that I am, I was curious to see the old film, and so I rented the DVD. As I watched, I decided that the movie had been underrated as a work of art, and that it made an important statement about the prejudice against Native Americans in the United States. What stood out for me in particular was how badly the women in the film discriminated against others—even women with no or little power—and how I did not want to grow up to become that kind of woman.

EXAMPLE 2 (WORK OF ART):

First paragraph: Carmen was stabbed. Tosca jumped to her death. And Leonore (*Fidelio*) rescued her imprisoned husband.

Second paragraph: Somehow, as a child, I grew up thinking that opera was a dull and outdated art form that had no modern-day relevance. But once I saw my first few live and fully-staged operas three years ago, I realized that there is no art form more emotionally riveting than opera. I became intrigued with this combination of music, art, and theater, and decided that opera composition was what I wanted to study in college.

PARAGRAPHS 3 AND 4: By the third paragraph, you should be describing what *you* did or what you accomplished in response to the work of art or person you've chosen for your essay. In other words, the third and fourth paragraphs should focus on anecdotes about *you*. Keep in mind that the college admissions office only wants to learn about *you*—not the movie, opera, politician, or writer. Paragraphs 3 and 4 should tell the reader everything you want the college administrators to know about you. Here is where you insert your best credentials while continuing the story (the ones you listed several pages back in this chapter).

Third and fourth paragraphs: Having never seen operas in my first thirteen years of life, I suddenly became an avid operagoer—an addict of sorts—sneaking off to Lincoln Center at every opportunity on the weekends of my sophomore year in high school. I was curious to see each and every production offered by the Metropolitan and the New York City Operas, sometimes attending both a matinee and an evening performance in the same day, sitting up in the top balconies.

Then one day, I realized that I would like to compose operas—with modern themes that would draw younger crowds to Lincoln Center someday—and to make a career of it. So I stopped attending operas and started intensive music composition lessons instead. Having taken years of music theory and piano at the Center Valley Music School, I was eligible for the New York Academy of Music's Young Composers Program. I applied and was immediately accepted. In my first year there, the arias I wrote sounded relatively primitive, but as I progressed, the Academy agreed to stage some of my better pieces, and I was awarded two vocal composition prizes. All the while, professional composers at the Academy gave me helpful feedback.

THE FIFTH PARAGRAPH: The last paragraph should have a nice conclusion—the upbeat ending, once again tying the person or artwork to you, reinforcing the influence that the person or artwork has had on you, and possibly mentioning how this relates to your college career.

Fifth paragraph: As a novice composer, I'm not yet ready for Lincoln Center or Kennedy Center or any of the nation's wonderful opera houses. But I've been inspired by the allure of Carmen, the resolve of Tosca, and the courage of Leonore—three opera heroines, who introduced me to the magic and power of opera. In their tradition, I'm excited to be exploring my own voice as a composer, a pursuit I'm eager to continue in college.

SECOND COMPLETED (PERSON) ESSAY EXAMPLE

First paragraph (Option 2, description): His personal home library was so vast that it was separated into "collections." He had a section devoted to poetry, and another to science fiction. There was a bookcase that held only plays, and a whole wall was devoted to fiction, with all of the books alphabetized by author.

Second paragraph (connecting the person to you): When I think of my grandfather, who passed away three years ago, I immediately think of his wonderful collection of books, and how he is the one solely responsible for my passion for literature. "Have you read this one?" he would ask, pulling out a paperback casually. Or "Wait till you read this one!" he'd say with such enthusiasm that I couldn't wait to see what literary adventures were in store.

Third and fourth paragraphs (continuing the story; revealing your best credentials): Before I knew it, I became engrossed in works by Melville, Dickens, Orwell, and Shakespeare, and names I had never heard in school like Anton Chekhov, Thomas Mann, Lincoln Steffens, Vincent Sheean, and Sinclair Lewis. In fact, he led me through a whole muckraker period, when I read book after book, which ultimately resulted in my passion for journalism and literature. Together we would enjoy wonderful discussions on some of the world's greatest literature. After all, he taught literature for most of his life in a public high school. He introduced me to poets like Percy Shelley, William Butler Yeats, and John Keating—names that had vanished from my high school curriculum decades before.

All of this literary exposure made me want to immerse myself further in the world of books and newspapers. Inspired by my grandfather, I wrote many articles for the high school newspaper, and submitted an investigatory piece on the town's recycling program to the local town weekly, which they said they're going to publish next month. I became active in the school's Book Club, and on the staff of the school literary magazine, and I volunteered (and still do) one day a week in the school library.

Fifth paragraph (the feel-good ending): My grandfather successfully passed on to me his passion for literature. He would be proud to know that I've continued reading plays, novels, and even poetry and biographies, many from his vast collection. I cherish the portions that my grandfather highlighted in yellow. I feel these special markings reveal what he found to be the essence of each of his prized books, and as I read his books today, it's as if he's still sharing his insights with me.

CONCLUSION

Regardless of which Common Application essay prompt you select—whether you focus on past experiences or achievements that have impacted you, issues of importance to you, or people or characters who have influenced you—the resulting essay you submit to colleges ultimately needs to include the same basic information. It must tell the college admissions officers your best credentials, explain those credentials in context, and give the colleges reasons to want to accept you over all the other thousands or tens of thousands of qualified applicants.

If you've followed the step-by-step process in this book, you should be quite an expert by now in the art of writing outstanding and appealing essays that win you offers of admission to colleges on the basis of who you really are. I congratulate you on your newly acquired skill and trust that there will be many opportunities in your education and career when the skill of writing an application essay or personal statement will come in handy.

FINAL NOTE
FROM THE AUTHOR

Congratulations on completing your essays!

I hope this book made the process of writing your essays much simpler and much more enjoyable for you. And I hope that by now, using this book, you have written at least one wonderful mini autobiography to share with colleges.

I have found over the years that many of my students really treasure their main essays as one-page stories—true episodes from their life—worth framing. I hope that you do too.

Feel free to return to this book for each essay that you write.

ACKNOWLEDGMENTS

I want to thank all of my students for sharing their stories, dreams, and essays with me, and for inspiring me to write this book. Through their essays, my students have shown me over the years an enormously rich diversity of talents, skills, academic passions, and aspirations, and I find it exciting to follow how those qualities translate into real-world contributions. I'm always amazed by how unique each student's interests are, and I believe strongly that everyone has special talents to contribute. To me, guiding students in the college essay process is about helping each student to find and envision how he or she will take the best advantage of the many opportunities that will be presented in the future. I especially enjoy that role.

I also want to thank the many college admissions officers, who, through their decisions and discussions with me, have helped me to understand the powerful role that application essays play—and what admissions committees look for in these essays. While I am grateful that my students have been so successful when it comes to college and grad school admission, I have also come to appreciate the inherent value of the self-evaluation process that accompanies the art of writing and submitting application essays. These essays generally require students to reflect on their own values, aspirations, experiences, academic passions, goals, and progress toward those goals—all under deadline pressure. I believe that this kind of personal introspection is very worthwhile and, if done properly, should be enjoyable and not grueling.

I am most appreciative of the people at Random House for helping to make this book happen. I thank my editor, Christina Duffy, for her thoughtful editing and enthusiasm, and Jane Von Mehren, Kim Hovey, Crystal Velasquez, Theresa Zoro, Brian McLendon, and Anne Watters.

I want to thank my outstanding agent, Susan Ginsburg, for her ever-insightful guidance, and her assistant, Bethany Strout, who is always so thoughtful and helpful.

And I especially want to thank my family and friends for their support and understanding while I focused my attention on writing this book.

ABOUT THE AUTHOR

The author understands the fear and urge to procrastinate. After all, she has helped thousands of students through the college application process, since she began advising students more than twelve years ago.

In addition to writing two books on college admissions, *What Colleges Don't Tell You (and Other Parents Don't Want You to Know)* and *What High Schools Don't Tell You (and Other Parents Don't Want You to Know)*, ELIZABETH WISSNER-GROSS has been leading successful Write-Your-Essay-in-Less-than-a-Day workshops and speaking at public and private schools across the United States. She has appeared on the *Today Show* (NBC), *The Morning Show with Mike & Juliet* (Fox News), *I on NY* (WPXN), and been heard on *Martha Stewart* radio (Sirius) and popular radio programs throughout the United States. She is a regular keynote speaker on CollegeWeekLive (online semiannual college fair that attracts more than 35,000 viewers/participants), and has appeared on panels sponsored by *The New York Times, Newsday, The World Journal* (Chinese), and the Columbia/Princeton Club of New York. In addition, she has been featured in articles in *The New York Times, Newsday, USA Today, The World Journal,* and many other publications throughout the United States.

As a private educational consultant, advocate, and strategist, she has helped her students win admission into the colleges of their dreams—even in these most competitive times—by working with individual students to help them develop their own academic interests and passions, and then having them write about their experiences. She advocates encouraging the individuality of each student and celebrating the gifts, talents, and diverse contributions that she believes every student has to offer.

Elizabeth Wissner-Gross graduated from Barnard College, where she studied Political Science and Education and graduated cum laude in 1975. She went on to Columbia University Graduate School of Journalism and received her MS in 1976, and then pursued additional graduate study at UCLA. She worked as a writer and editor at the *Daily News of Los Angeles*, Associated Press, and *Newsday*, taught journalism at New York area colleges and graduate programs, and has had articles published in hundreds of newspapers nationally and internationally including *The New York Times*, *Boston Herald*, and *Los Angeles Times*. She resides on Long Island, New York and in Connecticut. She has two sons; both attended MIT undergraduate and Harvard for PhDs.

You're invited to visit her website at CollegeEssayInADay.com.